DAVID H. FINKELSTEIN

Expression
and the Inner

HARVARD UNIVERSITY PRESS

Cambridge, Massachusetts, and London, England

First Harvard University Press paperback edition, 2008

Library of Congress Cataloging-in-Publication Data

Finkelstein, David H.
    Expression and the inner / David H. Finkelstein.
        p. cm.
    Includes bibliographical references and index.
    ISBN 978-0-674-01156-4 (cloth)
    ISBN 978-0-674-03044-2 (pbk.)
    1. Self-knowledge, theory of.   2. Self-presentation.   I. Title.

    BD438.5.F525 2003
    128'.2—dc21   2003056643

EXPRESSION AND THE INNER

Contents

Acknowledgments

Shortly after I took my present job at the University of Chicago, I found myself having coffee with Leonard Linsky, a renowned emeritus professor in my department. He asked what I was working on, and I told him that I was trying to complete a book manuscript that I'd been fussing with obsessively for years. He said, "You want my advice? Make it perfect. I didn't do that with *my* first book, and I regret it to this day." This conversation made a deep impression on me, and I resolved to avoid all contact with Leonard until my book was in print.

This *has* been a long time coming. Parts of the story I tell here go back to my Ph.D. thesis (1994), most notably the argument against new detectivism in Chapter 1 and the idea that first-person authority loses its puzzling aspect when we recognize that a speaker may, by stating that she is happy (or in pain or longing for a bath), both express her state of mind and say something true about it. In addition to Leonard, many people have helped me along the way.

My reading of Wittgenstein's late work has been influenced more by Jim Conant, Cora Diamond, and John McDowell than anyone else. I'd be indebted to the three of them for what they've written, even if there weren't so many conversations to thank them for. For a variety of reasons, this book would not have been possible without them. And I consider myself fortunate to count Jim, with whom I've discussed this material more than anyone else, among my colleagues here in Chicago.

Before I came to Chicago, I taught at Indiana University, where Paul Franks and Michael Morgan were colleagues and friends. Mike and I had lunch every Friday at the Uptown Café, where he ordered meat-loaf, told me about European intellectuals I'd never heard of, and chatted with me about the book I was writing. Over the course of many months, he read and commented insightfully on drafts of every chapter. Paul let me talk him through lengthy outlines of this material, all the while offering measured, knowledgeable responses in a reassuring British accent.

Samantha Fenno provided years of steadfast encouragement and much keen advice, both philosophical and editorial. This project owes more to her than I can say. Kimberly Keller read over some of this material with me at bad restaurants late at night, offering writing tips and leaving me with the happy impression that even a medievalist could find this stuff interesting.

Stanley Cavell, Jim Conant, Cora Diamond, Anne Eaton, Jay Elliott, Jennifer Hornsby, and Barry Stroud read drafts and provided comments that proved extremely valuable through the months spent on revisions. The manuscript was much improved thanks to their feedback. More recently, Shadi Bartsch let me read almost all of what's here to her aloud. Her astute comments and questions occasioned numerous last-minute revisions that made the text more readable and coherent.

Finally, I want to gratefully acknowledge my dog, Kita, who lay beside my desk at school through many late nights of writing, seeing to it that if a squirrel should somehow secure a key to my office, he wouldn't dare to use it.*

This book is dedicated to my father, Robert Finkelstein, my first and longest-standing philosophical interlocutor, and to my mother, Thelma Finkelstein, who—having long ago reconciled herself to the fact that I won't be attending medical school *or* law school—still hopes that I'll learn to dress a little better. I don't know how to describe how loving and supportive they've both been.

*   *   *

In writing this, I've borrowed from and modified stretches of text of varying lengths from three of my published papers: "On the Distinc-

---

* When I need a gender-neutral third-person singular pronoun, I'll sometimes use "he" and sometimes "she." I don't mean to suggest that Kita was not on guard against intrusive *female* squirrels.

tion between Conscious and Unconscious States of Mind," *American Philosophical Quarterly* 36 (April 1999): 79–100; "Wittgenstein on Rules and Platonism," in *The New Wittgenstein*, edited by Alice Crary and Rupert Reed (London: Routledge, 2000), pp. 53–73; and "Wittgenstein's 'Plan for the treatment of psychological concepts,'" in *Wittgenstein in America*, edited by Timothy McCarthy and Sean Stidd (Oxford, 2001), pp. 215–236. I'm grateful to the publishers.

I have, in a couple of publications, made reference to an unpublished paper of mine called "Detection, Expression, and First-Person Authority." Most of that paper has made its way into Chapter 1 of this book.

I'm very grateful to Lindsay Waters and Thomas Wheatland at Harvard University Press for their encouragement and patience, among other things, and to my copyeditor, Kate Schmit, for being so good at her job.

And Leonard, I'm sorry. Let's have coffee again soon.

EXPRESSION AND THE INNER

Introduction

Your friend Max tells you that he has, by mistake, bought tickets to two concerts that are taking place at the same time on the same evening. "Now," he complains, "I'll have to choose between Yo-Yo Ma and Bob Dylan." A couple of days later, you ask Max's wife if he's resolved his musical dilemma. She says that he intends to sell the Dylan ticket and attend the Yo-Yo Ma concert. That afternoon, you run into Max and congratulate him on his choice. He says, "Sarah must have misunderstood me. I may need to be out of town that weekend, in which case I'll try to sell both tickets, but if I can, I intend to see Dylan."

Sarah knows Max *very* well. If you wanted to find out what size shirt he wears or how long he goes between haircuts, you'd do better to ask her than him. Nonetheless, it doesn't even occur to you to think that Max, rather than Sarah, might be mistaken about which ticket he intends to use. It doesn't occur to you to ask Max for evidence supporting his assertion that he intends to see Dylan. (And if you *were* to ask for evidence, he would think you were joking.) Indeed, it is difficult to imagine how Max could be mistaken about which concert he means to attend. This isn't to say that he's never wrong about what he intends. But it's hard to see how he could be wrong in *this* case, and, as a rule, if you want to know what Max intends, he's the best person to ask. He is, we might say, the best *authority* concerning his intentions. And not only his intentions; Max speaks with what seems to be a similar sort of authority about his own hopes, fears, desires, beliefs, moods, emotions, sensations, and passing thoughts.

1

Philosophers and psychologists have expressed a range of opinions concerning how this sort of authority ought to be understood. Quite a number of these can be counted as versions of what I shall call "detectivism." A detectivist would try to explain the authority with which a person speaks about his own mental life by appeal to a process that enables him to *find out* about it, to detect his own hopes, fears, emotions, etc., and thereby render them conscious. Typically, this consciousness is understood as involving a kind of inward observation or perception. Most detectivists would hold that Max is in a better position than Sarah to speak about *his* intentions because he enjoys something like the best view of them.

Detectivism has had many adherents, my former self among them. That some version of it must be correct—that detectivism must provide the right framework in which to think about consciousness and first-person authority—can seem so obvious, so uncontroversial, that it is very often taken for granted by both philosophers and psychologists. This book grew out of my becoming convinced that no detectivist could succeed in explaining either the kind of authority with which Max speaks about his intention to attend the Dylan concert or that by virtue of which such an intention is rightly said to be conscious.

In Chapter 1, it is argued that detectivism should be rejected. If we do reject it, how might we think about our example? According to the sort of position discussed in Chapter 2, Max should not be understood as judging that he intends to see Dylan on the basis of his having detected that this is what he intends. Rather, in judging that he intends to see Dylan, Max *makes it the case* that this is what he intends. The point is not that Max's self-ascription of intention *causes* an intention to arise; it is that his intending to see Dylan *consists* (at least to some extent) in his taking himself to have this intention. According to what I'll be calling "constitutivism," first-person authority comes to this: often, when someone judges himself to intend, believe, hope, or fear a particular thing, he thereby makes it the case that he does.

I'll claim that neither detectivism nor constitutivism can be the right approach toward understanding first-person authority or consciousness. This might appear to leave me in an awkward position. After all, there can be only so many broad, sensible options for thinking about these things. Surely, we are able to speak as we do about our own mental states and events either because we discover them in ourselves or because we somehow constitute or construct them or because we do a bit of both—sometimes discovering and sometimes constructing. By the end of Chapter 2, I'll have committed myself to rejecting all three horns of this trilemma. In Chapter 3, it will become apparent that there *is* one more sensible option. There, I shall discuss an account of inner awareness due to John McDowell that manages to blur the line between discovery and construction. McDowell charts a course between detectivism and constitutivism and, in so doing, brings together the virtues of both. This "middle path account of inner awareness" (as I'll call it) suggests that the way to understand the relations we bear to a significant range of our own inner goings-on is as involving something *between* discovery and construction. By the end of Chapter 3, i.e., the end of Part I, I'll have rejected this option as well.

∗   ∗   ∗

In his late work, Ludwig Wittgenstein expresses opposition to detectivism. He writes:

> Other people cannot be said to learn of my sensations *only* from behaviour,—for *I* cannot be said to learn of them. I *have* them.   (*PI* §246)

> Does it make sense to ask "How do you know that you believe?"—and is the answer: "I know it by introspection"?
>   In *some* cases it will be possible to say some such thing, in most not. (*PI* §587)

> Psychological verbs characterized by the fact that the third person of the present is to be verified by observation, the first person not. (*Z* §472)

> What I do is not, of course, to identify my sensation by criteria: but to repeat an expression. But this is not the *end* of the language-game: it is the beginning.
>   But isn't the beginning the sensation—which I describe?—Perhaps this word "describe" tricks us here. I say "I describe my state of mind" and "I describe my room." You need to call to mind the differences between the language-games.   (*PI* §290)

Remarks such as these appear often in Wittgenstein's writings. In my view, they merit our attention because—not to put too fine a point on this—they are, by and large, right. But, as is illustrated by the final quotation in the above list, they are not always easy to understand. Beginning in Chapter 2 and continuing off and on through the book, I'll be discussing two opposed readings of what Wittgenstein has to say about psychological self-ascription, readings that have been put forward by McDowell and by Crispin Wright. Each seems to think that we can learn from Wittgenstein how best to understand a subject's relations to her own inner states and events. While I agree with this assessment of what might be gained from the right sort of engagement with Wittgenstein, I believe that both Wright and McDowell misrepresent his thinking on this topic.

Wright defends constitutivism and suggests that we read Wittgenstein as a constitutivist. McDowell, who argues for the middle path account of inner awareness, takes Wittgenstein to recommend the middle path. One of my goals in Part II will be to offer a reading of Wittgenstein that is, on the one hand, more faithful to his texts than either Wright's reading or McDowell's and, on the other hand, suggestive of a more satisfactory account of first-person authority and consciousness. My main goal will be to articulate and defend this account—an account according to which the relation a person bears to one of her own attitudes, emotions, or sensations is not, typically, well thought of as a matter of discovery *or* construction *or* a little bit of discovery plus a little bit of construction *or* something that somehow lies between discovery and construction.

*   *   *

Wittgenstein writes:

> But how does the person in whom it goes on know which event the process is the expectation of? For he does not seem to be in uncertainty about it. It is not as if he observed a mental or other condition and formed a conjecture about its cause. He may well say: "I don't know whether it is only this expectation that makes me so uneasy today"; but he will not say: "I don't know whether this state of mind, in which I now am, is the expectation of an explosion or of something else."
>
> The statement "I am expecting a bang at any moment" is an *expression* of expectation. This verbal reaction is the movement of the pointer, which shows the object of expectation.   (*Z* §53)

There is here a rejection of detectivism followed, in the last couple of sentences, by a positive, if somewhat confusingly elaborated,[1] suggestion concerning how we should think about a self-ascription of expectation. We find this suggestion, or something similar, again and again in Wittgenstein's late writings. He proposes that we understand self-ascriptions of hope (*PI* §585), irritation (*LWPP2*, 70), pain (*PI* §244), indeed all manner of psychological self-ascriptions (*Z* §472), as *expressions,* or as akin to expressions—akin, that is, to cries of pain, amused smiles, and the like.

This proposal tends not to be taken very seriously. Rather, it is widely thought to show that Wittgenstein held, or perhaps merely flirted with, a patently unsatisfactory position according to which such utterances as "I'm expecting a bang" and "I have a headache" are—like smiles, winces, and wordless cries—bits of behavior that are neither true nor false. According to this sort of "expressivism," self-ascriptions or avowals of mental states should be understood as expressions *rather than* assertions. Imagine that after Max says to you, "I intend to see the Dylan concert," you learn that he did not ever so intend; moreover, he wasn't self-deceived or otherwise confused about what he intended to do. Given the expressivist position, you could not rightly complain that he *lied* to you—that he deliberately told you something he knew to be false—for, according to this position, Max's words were neither true nor false.

Now, the proposal that we understand psychological self-ascriptions in this way *is* difficult to take seriously. But, as I'll urge in Chapter 4, it isn't Wittgenstein's proposal. His point is not that we should hear a remark like Max's as an expression *rather than* an assertion. To call attention to the fact that some utterance is, or is akin to, an expression needn't be to deny that it is an assertion as well. Indeed, on the assumption that Max is not deliberately misleading you, it would surely be correct to say the following: *in* asserting that he intends to see the Dylan concert, Max expresses his intention to see it; he both expresses his state of mind and says something true about it. Wittgenstein suggests not that mental state self-ascriptions lack truth values, but that a failure to attend to what might be called their expressive *dimension* leads one into philosophical confusion.

1. I'll discuss "the movement of the pointer" in Chapter 4.

I believe that this suggestion *is* worth taking seriously—moreover, that we stand to gain a good deal by investigating the *ways* in which a self-ascription of, say, pain or joy is akin to a pained wince or a joyful smile. In Chapters 5 and 6, the book's last two chapters, I'll try to show that such an investigation can help us think about not only first-person authority but, among other things, (1) the distinction between conscious psychological states and unconscious ones, (2) how sentience is related to sapience, and (3) how our minds are like, and unlike, the minds of nonlinguistic animals.

PART I

Detectivism and Constitutivism

CHAPTER 1

Detectivism

If you want to know what I think, feel, imagine, or intend, I am a good person—indeed, usually the best person—to ask. It is sometimes said that I enjoy a kind of authority when I talk about what, loosely speaking, might be called my own states of mind—when I say, e.g., "My head hurts," "I was worried about you," or "I intend to arrive early." When people don't accept my mental state self-ascriptions at face value, it is generally because they take me to be insincere rather than mistaken.

It is easy to be struck by such facts and, once struck, to find oneself inclined to ask questions about them: How is it that we are able to state our own thoughts and feelings so easily, accurately, and authoritatively? How is describing one's own state of mind different from describing someone else's? This chapter concerns a natural and widespread approach to answering such questions—an approach that I call "detectivism." A detectivist is someone who believes that a person's ability to speak about her own states of mind as easily, accurately, and authoritatively as she does may be explained by appeal to a process by which she *finds out* about them. According to detectivism, I am able to state my own thoughts and feelings because they are conscious, and they're conscious thanks to a cognitive process by which I have detected their presence. If I'm in an especially good position to say what's in *my* mind, it is because this cognitive process provides me with better epistemic access to my mental states than other people have to them.

In this chapter, I shall try to persuade you that no form of detectivism provides us with the materials we need in order to understand first-person authority. In what immediately follows, I'll trace some of detectivism's history, focusing in particular on two detectivist positions set out by Bertrand Russell in 1912 and in 1921. These positions of Russell's will serve as representative versions of what I shall call "old" and "new" detectivism.

1.1. Old Detectivism

Most detectivists have thought that we can say what's on our minds thanks to a kind of inward observation or perception. Auguste Comte argues that such a view presupposes an incoherent conception of the mind's relation to its own states. In his *Cours de Philosophie Positive,* Comte ridicules the experimental psychologists of his day for thinking that human reasoning could be studied by inward observation:

> [A]s for examining . . . intellectual phenomena as they appear, this is manifestly impossible. A thinking individual cannot divide himself into two, one half reasoning, and the other watching it reason. The observed and the observing organ become identical in this case. How could observation take place?
>
> The so-called psychological method therefore is in principle invalid. And consider to what absolutely contradictory antics it leads! On the one hand you are told to insulate yourself, as much as possible, from every external sensation, above all you must refrain from intellectual work; for if you were to do the simplest sum, what would become of *internal* observation? On the other hand, after having by dint of precautions attained the state of intellectual sleep, you must busy yourself contemplating the operations taking place in your mind, when nothing at all is taking place in it! Our posterity will doubtless one day see these pretensions transferred to the comic stage.   (Comte 1974, 32)

John Stuart Mill replies to Comte on behalf of introspective psychology:

> In the first place, M. Comte might be referred to experience, and to the writings of his countryman M. Cardaillac and our own Sir William Hamilton for proof that the mind can not only be conscious of, but attend to, more than one, and even a considerable number of impressions at once . . . Secondly, it might have occurred to M. Comte that a

fact may be studied through the medium of memory, not at the very moment of our perceiving it, but the moment after: and this is really the mode in which our best knowledge of our intellectual acts is generally acquired. We reflect on what we have been doing when the act is past, but when its impression in the memory is still fresh. Unless in one of these ways, we could not have acquired the knowledge, which nobody denies us to have, of what passes in our own minds . . . Whatever we are directly aware of, we can directly observe.   (Mill 1961, 63–64).

Mill's point is not merely that we perceive our own reasonings on odd occasions, e.g., when asked to by psychologists. It is rather that our ordinary, moment-by-moment awareness of what "passes in our own minds" is due to a kind of inward perception (plus memory). A detectivist thinks that our ordinary consciousness of, at least, some significant range of mental states is explained by the fact that we are able to perceive—or anyway, detect—their presence. Mill's reply to Comte is cited approvingly by many of the leading lights in the succeeding generation of philosophers, including Franz Brentano and William James, both of whom defend related positions.[1]

For all of its radical critique of previous philosophy, early analytic philosophy mostly adopts a broadly detectivist conception of a subject's relations to his own inner goings-on. Within the development of analytic philosophy, it is important to distinguish two distinct forms of detectivism, each of which (like so much else in analytic philosophy) can be traced back to a phase in the thought of Bertrand Russell.

In 1912, in *The Problems of Philosophy,* Russell distinguishes between our knowledge of physical objects and our knowledge of the sense-data that make up their appearances. He describes the latter as "things with which I have acquaintance, things immediately known to me just as they are" (Russell 1912, 47). By contrast, when I see or touch a physical object, I am aware of its existence only indirectly—only insofar as I have inferred that such a thing would be the most likely cause of my current visual or tactile sense-data.

According to Russell, we know not only our sense-data but also our own mental goings-on by acquaintance.[2] He writes:

---

1. See Brentano 1973, 35; James 1890, 189.

2. According to Russell's sense-datum theory, sense-data are not mental—or anyway are "not known to be mental" (Russell 1992, 5; also see Russell 1912, 38–43).

When I desire food, I may be aware of my desire for food; thus 'my desiring food' is an object with which I am acquainted. Similarly we may
be aware of our feeling pleasure or pain, and generally of the events
which happen in our minds. This kind of acquaintance, which may be
called self-consciousness, is the source of all our knowledge of mental
things.   (1912, 49)

A couple of pages later, Russell introduces the expression "inner
sense." He says, "We have acquaintance in sensation with the data of
the outer senses, and in introspection with the data of what may be
called the inner sense—thoughts, feelings, desires, etc." (1912, 51). A
guiding thought of almost all detectivists is that there is an important
parallel between my relation to the physical objects before my eyes and
my relation to my own states of mind. The expression "inner sense" is
meant to capture this parallel. Russell, however, also takes there to be
significant disanalogies between the inner and outer senses. (It would
be misleading to say, "Russell thinks of self-knowledge as involving a
sixth sense—a faculty just like seeing and hearing, only aimed in a different direction.") Here is one of the disanalogies: while inner and
outer senses have acquaintance in common, acquaintance is all there
is to inner cognition, while it is supplemented by inference in outer
perception. If we call physical objects the *termini* of the outer senses—
because the purpose of the outer senses is to inform us about physical
objects—then we can say that according to Russell, the termini of, say,
vision are not its immediate objects. Vision's termini, e.g., the trees
and cars that I see out my window, are explanatory posits. By contrast,
the termini of the inner sense—thoughts, feelings, and attitudes—are
its immediate objects and are experienced directly.

A second, related respect in which inner and outer cognition differ according to Russell lies in the fact that we know our own mental
states *better* than we know external objects, with greater—indeed, complete—certainty: "[T]he certainty of our knowledge of our own experiences does not have to be limited in any way to allow for exceptional
cases" (1912, 19). The inner sense provides us with perfect knowledge
of inner objects. No outer sense yields this kind of access to physical
objects.

So while Russell's talk of *inner sense* suggests that we know our own
minds by a kind of perceptual mechanism, we should appreciate how
different inwardly detecting our own desires is from seeing or hearing

physical objects. We might say that for Russell at this stage, the mechanism by which we know our own minds is *perceptual* only in an extended or metaphorical sense.[3] According to this kind of detectivism, introspecting is far more different from seeing, hearing, tasting, smelling, or feeling than these are from one another. I'll call this kind of detectivism, according to which we know our own minds via an, as it were, *sui generis* perceptual process, "old detectivism." The old detectivist claims that this process provides me, and only me, with a kind of access to my mental states that is complete, infallible, and more direct than my access to the keyboard on which I'm presently typing.

*   *   *

Old detectivism makes room for a thought that may seem intuitively compelling, viz., that when I say, "I'm in pain," or, "I want a sandwich," something is going on that is fundamentally different from what occurs when I describe another person's state of mind or when I describe the state of my office. However appealing this thought may be, old detectivism accommodates it at too great a cost. The old detectivist's conception of the mind is subject to a pair of related and mutually sustaining pressures: he is forced to picture the mind (1) as an immaterial organ and (2) as epistemically cut off from goings-on outside it. I'll say just a little bit about each of these pressures in order to make intelligible the transition that we find in the work of Russell and others from old detectivism to what I'll be calling "new detectivism." (In so doing, I'll be leading you over a terrain whose features may be familiar to you. We should cover this ground, if only briefly, in order to appreciate how it is that new detectivism has come to appear superior to old detectivism. Soon, I shall argue that this appearance is illusory.)

(1) The old detectivist is under pressure to picture the mind as an immaterial organ for a number of reasons. One is that the mechanism of inner sense that he postulates is supernaturally reliable. I might say of a particularly obvious barn, "You can't miss it"; but a barn, no mat-

---

3. Russell's extension of the language of perception to relations of acquaintance is typical of sense-datum theorists. H. H. Price, for example, writes, "Data of this special sort are called *sense-data*. And the acquaintance with them is conveniently called *sensing*" (Price 1932, 3). (Price goes on to compare sense-data with "the data of the detective," saying that the detective's data are unlike sense-data in that they are "really the result of inference" [1932, 4].)

ter how large and obvious, might be missed by someone who was distracted or whose eyes were not functioning properly. According to old detectivism, mental items are such that they can *never* go unnoticed by the subject to whom they appear. Unlike eyes or ears, the old detectivist's inner sense *cannot* break down or fail to function. Could such a mechanism be made of mere matter?[4]

(2) One source of dissatisfaction with old detectivism lies in its association with dualism. But just as significant is the fact that old detectivism tends toward scepticism about the external world and about other minds. In *The Problems of Philosophy*, Russell claims that we may justifiably infer that there are external objects because this hypothesis provides the *simplest* way to account for our sense-data: "[E]very principle of simplicity urges us to adopt the natural view, that there really are objects other than ourselves and our sense-data which have an existence not dependent upon our perceiving them" (1912, 24).[5] How should we assess this claim? Consider my present situation—one that I might be pretheoretically inclined to describe as follows: "I am looking at the lamp next to my computer." According to Russell, I have posited the existence of an object (a lamp) external to my present sense-data in order to account for some of them. Is this the simplest way to understand my experience? Why is it simpler to hypothesize that the sense-data in question are caused by one object rather than by two or by many? Am I supposed to be moved by ontological parsimony at this point? Wouldn't the most parsimonious course be to refrain entirely from positing entities that lie outside my experience?[6]

Knowledge of other minds presents the old detectivist with further problems. According to Russell, I learn about the mind of another via *two* problematic inferences. First, I must establish that he—or rather,

4. Lycan (1996) points to the connection between super-reliability and immateriality when he writes (on behalf of new detectivism), "[S]ince an internal monitor is a physical device, and so subject to malfunction, it might report falsely" (17).

5. Russell loses faith in this sort of appeal to simplicity shortly after writing *The Problems of Philosophy*. In unpublished writing from 1912, he admits that we would have grounds for thinking that "of two hypotheses which both fit the data, the simpler is more likely to be true" only if we knew that "the universe had been created for the purpose of delighting mathematicians" (quoted on p. 386 of Hylton 1990).

6. In a paper written in 1914 called "The relation of sense-data to physics," Russell comes around to the view that we ought to refrain from positing objects beyond the sense-data. He writes: "[I]nferred entities should, whenever this can be done, be similar to those whose existence is given, rather than, like the Kantian *Ding an sich*, some-

his body—exists. This is a matter of positing an external cause (the "simplest" explanation) of some of my sense-data. Second, on the basis of analogical reasoning, I infer that the movements of his body are accompanied by thoughts and feelings of the sort I have when my body moves in similar ways. Even a sense-datum theorist who was not terribly bothered by the first inference might find it difficult to countenance the second.[7]

1.2. New Detectivism

Eventually, in the face of such difficulties, Russell's detectivism changes dramatically. To see how this goes, it will help to consider the analysis of desire that he puts forward in 1921, in *The Analysis of Mind*. What a desire is, Russell says there, is any mental occurrence that involves "discomfort"—where a mental occurrence's involving discomfort consists in the fact that it causes an organism to engage in "movements tending to produce some more or less definite change involving the cessation of the occurrence" (Russell 1921, 71; see p. 75 for a summary of the view). Hunger, for example, is a feeling that causes an organism to engage in restless movements that are likely to lead to its eating. That hunger is a desire *to eat* consists in the fact that upon eating, the restless activity ceases. "The thing which will bring a restless condition to an end is said to be what is desired" (1921, 32).[8]

---

thing wholly remote from the data which nominally support the inference" (Russell 1917, 116). Rather than infer the existence of physical objects wholly unlike sense-data, Russell here suggests what he takes to be a more conservative inference. We should infer that the items we call sense-data sometimes exist even when they are not present to a mind. He uses the term "sensibilia" to refer to these items without presupposing that they are data for a mind. (Sense-data are sensibilia that happen to be present to a mind.) Having concluded that our immediate acquaintance is with items that may exist unbeknownst to anyone, Russell argues that the physical world is made up of such items. Sensibilia (and so sense-data) are, he thinks, physical entities; indeed, they constitute the subject matter of physics.

7. Russell himself expresses doubt about the argument from analogy in his *Theory of Knowledge: The 1913 Manuscript*, when he suggests that we treat the existence of other minds as a "working hypothesis" (Russell 1992, 14).

8. Wittgenstein makes fun of this analysis of desire: "If I wanted to eat an apple, and someone punched me in the stomach, taking away my appetite, then it was this punch that I originally wanted" (*PR*, 64; see also *PI* §440). Later versions of new detectivism prove to be less vulnerable to one-line refutations. (To be fair to Russell, he does try to answer what amounts to this criticism on p. 64 of *The Analysis of Mind*.)

Given this story about what desires are, how do we know our own? Russell writes:

> "Conscious" desire . . . consists of desire in the sense hitherto discussed, together with a true belief as to its "purpose," i.e. as to the state of affairs that will bring quiescence with cessation of the discomfort. If our theory of desire is correct, belief as to its purpose may very well be erroneous, since only experience can show what causes a discomfort to cease. (1921, 72)

> I believe that the discovery of our own motives can only be made by the same process by which we discover other people's, namely, the process of observing our actions and inferring the desire which could prompt them. A desire is "conscious" when we have told ourselves that we have it. (1921, 31)

I know what I desire by making an inference—based on past experience with my behavior—concerning what it is that will bring my restless activity to an end. As Russell says, this inference may well be erroneous. Indeed, "Our spontaneous, unsophisticated beliefs, whether as to ourselves or as to the outer world, are always extremely rash and very liable to error. The acquisition of caution is equally necessary and equally difficult in both directions" (1921, 122). What Russell commits himself to is not the relatively banal claim that we *occasionally* learn what we desire by making a fallible inference from our own behavior. It is, rather, that our ordinary awareness of our own desires has this character. According to Russell, whenever I have a conscious desire, I have made an inference about myself. Compare this position with his earlier account of self-knowledge. In 1912, in *The Problems of Philosophy*, his view had been that I know my desires thanks to an inner sense that provides me with a kind of access to them that is complete, infallible, and more direct than my access to any external object. Now, in 1921, Russell claims that I know my desires by the same sort of fallible theorizing that allows me to learn the desires of others.

I call this sort of position—one according to which a mental state is conscious by virtue of an awareness of it that is roughly on a par with the sort of awareness one has to external states and events—"new detectivism." In *The Analysis of Mind*, Russell takes our access to our own desires to be on a par with our access to external states and events that we learn about *via inference*. This makes him an *atypical* new detectivist. Most new detectivists take our awareness of our own states of mind to be roughly on a par with our access to external states and events that we learn about perceptually. They claim that we find out about our own mental states via a kind of inward observation or perception—a very different *sort* of inward observation or perception, however, from that invoked by old detectivists. Recall that according to old detectivism, we learn about our own states of mind by a process that can be called "perceptual" only in an extended or metaphorical sense. An old detectivist's inner sense is a supernaturally reliable detection mechanism that provides a person with a kind of access to mental states that is more direct and certain than the sort of access that seeing or hearing could ever provide. New detectivists typically seek to domesticate this story—to render it less Cartesian and more naturalistic—by construing our awareness of our own mental states as involving a species of ordinary, garden-variety perception. Like Russell in 1912, new detectivists sometimes speak of an "inner sense" (or "internal sense" or "inner eye") that allows us to perceive what's going on in our own minds. Unlike Russell's employment of this expression, a new detectivist's use of it should be understood, as it were, literally (or, at least, much less metaphorically)—as referring to a faculty that is on all fours with seeing and hearing, only directed at states and events that happen to be inside the mind. Thus, David Armstrong writes, "By sense-perception we become aware of current physical happenings in our environment and our body. By inner sense we become aware of current happenings in our own mind" (Armstrong 1968, 95); William Lycan defends what he calls the "inner-sense theory" according to which "conscious awareness is the successful operation of an internal scanner or monitor that outputs second-order representations of first-order psychological states" (Lycan 1996, 31); and D. H. Mellor writes, "I can know so much about my own beliefs because I happen to have an internal sense that informs me of them" (Mellor 1977–78, 100). Paul Churchland provides a nice statement of this sort of perceptual new detectivism:

> [S]elf-consciousness . . . is just a species of perception: *self-perception*. It is not perception of one's foot with one's eyes, for example, but is rather the perception of one's internal states with what we may call (largely in ignorance) one's faculty of introspection. Self-consciousness is thus no more (and no less) mysterious than perception gener-

ally. It is just directed internally rather than externally.   (Churchland 1984, 74)

Finally, expressions of this sort of new detectivism also appear in contemporary psychology. Nicholas Humphrey, a neuropsychologist, writes:

> It is as if I, like every other human being, possess a kind of 'inner eye,' which looks in on my brain and tells me why and how I'm acting in the way I am—providing me with what amounts to a plain man's guide to my own mind.   (Humphrey 1986, 87)

*   *   *

The new detectivist looks back on his old detectivist predecessors and thinks: "They were right, of course, to claim that what brings a mental state to consciousness is its being detected. But they were wrong to think this detection such a special business. Ever since Descartes, philosophers have been overly impressed by the subject's *special* relation to his own states of mind. There's nothing so special about this relation. We are able to talk about our own pains, fears, intentions, etc. thanks to the fact that we learn about them, and we learn about them in the same sorts of ways that we learn about the goings-on around us. We happen to have been equipped by evolution with mechanisms that are sensitive to, and inform us about, the goings-on in our own minds."[9] I believe that this gets things precisely backwards. Old detectivists were *right* in thinking that the subject's relation to his own mental states is special. Their *mistake* lay in understanding this as a matter of detection.

That this was where their mistake lay is not easy to show. Most of the anti-detectivist arguments that one finds in the philosophical literature (both contemporary and not so contemporary) can be answered by a smart new detectivist. Consider, for example, the following from a book by John Searle:

---

9. Armstrong writes: "[F]or the Cartesian tradition the current contents of the mind all intimate themselves to an infallible faculty. What glory for inner sense! But, of course, to many, especially to those with a naturalist bent, it all seems too good to be true. The proper reaction, I believe, . . . is to scale down inner sense to a faculty like any other human faculty of knowledge, a faculty which fails to discern much, and which can fall into error" (Armstrong and Malcolm 1984, 123).

[W]e seem to get a vicious regress if we hold that the phenomenon of bringing unconscious states to consciousness consists in perceiving previously unconscious mental phenomena . . . For the question then arises: What about the act of perceiving—is this a mental phenomenon? If so . . . it would appear that for me to become conscious of that act, I would need some higher-level act of perceiving of my act of perceiving. (Searle 1992, 171)

Someone who thinks that mental phenomena become conscious by being inwardly perceived could reply to Searle's argument as follows: "Even if it's true that in order for an act of inward perceiving to become conscious, a higher-level act of perceiving is necessary, this does not imply any vicious regress. Some mental phenomena, including some acts of inward perceiving, are *not* conscious;[10] they are not themselves inwardly perceived.[11] A vicious regress would threaten only if it were claimed that *all* mental phenomena are inwardly perceived."[12]

1.3. A Dialogue

One source of difficulty in trying to argue against new detectivism lies in the variety of forms that it can take: an anti-detectivist argument

10. In his *New Essays on Human Understanding,* Leibniz has Theophilus say: "[I]t is impossible that we should always reflect explicitly on all our thoughts; for if we did, the mind would reflect on each reflection, *ad infinitum,* without ever being able to move on to a new thought" (Leibniz 1981, II, i, §19). The word "all" is doing real work here; no such objection can be raised against the claim that we reflect explicitly on *many* of our thoughts.

11. Armstrong (1968) writes: "If we make the materialist identification of mental states with material states of the brain, we can say that introspection is a self-scanning process in the brain. The scanning operation may itself be scanned, and so on, but we must in the end reach an unscanned scanner. However, the unscanned scanner is not a logically unscannable scanner, for it is always possible to imagine a further scanning operation" (324).

12. New detectivists are committed to the idea that someone's mechanism of inner sense—like the mechanisms that enable a person to see and hear—could conceivably break down. Thus, another strategy for arguing against new detectivism would be to try to show that this sort of breakdown is not conceivable. Sydney Shoemaker pursues this strategy in several of his papers (e.g., Shoemaker 1988 and 1994); he argues that we cannot so much as imagine what he calls "self-blindness." I criticize this argument in my Postscript and, at greater length, in Finkelstein 1999b.

that speaks against one version of new detectivism may do nothing to undermine a slightly different version. It is partly for this reason that the argument against new detectivism I'll be presenting in this section takes the form of a dialogue between a new detectivist *(ND)* and an anti-detectivist *(AD)*. The dialogue form encourages us to imagine a new detectivist who reformulates his position repeatedly in response to criticism.

> *AD:* Tell me if I'm getting this right. Unlike the old detectivists, who took us to be perfect detectors of our own mental states, you new detectivists admit the possibility of mental states that go unnoticed by their subject.
>
> *ND:* That's right. If we're going to say that we detect our own thoughts and feelings, we have to admit the possibility of our failing to notice some of them. And we do fail to notice lots of them.[13] When a person is *unconsciously* angry or jealous, she's failed to detect the presence of one of her own mental states. I speak with first-person authority about my states of mind not because I have *perfect* epistemic access to them, but simply because, as a rule, I have *better* epistemic access to them than other people have.
>
> *AD:* Well then, the first step toward seeing what's wrong with your way of accounting for first-person authority is to mark the distinction between two issues: whether or not some mental state is *known* to its subject and whether or not it is *conscious*. I might know that I am angry, even though my anger is unconscious. Imagine that my therapist, whom I trust and have good reason to trust, tells me that I've been unconsciously jealous of my sister since I was a child. I might, thereby, learn a fact about myself— that I harbor unconscious jealousy—without becoming consciously jealous.
>
> A way to put this point would be to say that there's a distinction between "conscious *of*" and "conscious*ly*." I may be con-

---

13. Armstrong (1968) writes: "When we perceive, there are many (indeed innumerable) features of our environment that we do not perceive. In the same way, when we are aware of our current mental states, there are mental states and features of mental states of which we are unaware. These are mental states or features of mental states of which we are unconscious" (326).

scious *of,* i.e., aware of, my jealousy without being conscious*ly* jealous. For me to be consciously jealous—i.e., for my jealousy to *be* conscious and not merely something I am conscious *of*—it does not suffice for me merely to *know* that I am jealous.[14]

ND: So there's a distinction between someone's knowing that he's jealous and his being consciously jealous. What bearing do you take this to have on my way of explaining first-person authority?

AD: Let me say a little bit about first-person authority, about the sort of phenomenon it is; then, I'll answer your question. Consider a case in which I speak about someone else's state of mind. Imagine I tell you that a mutual friend of ours—call her Ruth—is angry with her uncle. You might just accept my assertion, or you might ask me to provide evidence in support of it. Whether or not you ask for evidence, if my claim about Ruth is responsible, then I should be able to provide some. It could be that I saw Ruth shouting at her uncle or slamming a door in his face, or perhaps she told me that she was furious with him.

Imagine now instead that I tell you that I'm angry with my uncle. One difference between this sort of case and one in which I'm speaking about another person's anger is that here, it would be odd for you to ask me for evidence supporting my assertion without your having some genuine reason for supposing that I wasn't angry with my uncle. But let's imagine that you ask anyway; you simply insist that I cite some evidence supporting my claim that I'm angry with my uncle.

I might be able to provide evidence. Perhaps I remember recently shouting at my uncle or slamming a door in his face. But such incidents seem beside the point, and whether or not I am able to think of any it would be reasonable and natural for me to reply: "What do you mean? I'm just really angry with him." There's an asymmetry between speaking about someone else's anger and speaking about one's own. I am able to ascribe mental states to myself responsibly without being able to cite evidence in support of the ascriptions. This is a central feature of first-person authority.

ND: And so?

14. For further discussion of this point, see §5.4.

AD: Notice that we don't speak with that sort of authority about our own mental states unless they are *conscious.* Imagine that I say, "I'm unconsciously angry with my uncle," whereupon you ask what the evidence is for this assertion. Here, I cannot reasonably respond: "What do you mean? I'm just really angry with him." If someone's mental state is not conscious (i.e., if he's not consciou*sly* angry, afraid, intending to visit Paris, believing that his love is true, or whatever), then although he may be aware of it, he cannot speak about it with first-person authority. The claims that I make about my unconscious states of mind are only as good as the evidence that stands behind them.

And now, I can say what's wrong with your position. In order for me to speak with first-person authority about some mental state, it's not enough that I *know* about it; it must be conscious. What you can *explain,* however, simply by positing a mechanism that enables us to detect our own states of mind is, at most, our *knowledge* of them. You cannot thereby explain how it is that we come to be consciously angry (or afraid, or intending to visit Paris . . .). And since merely knowing one's own state of mind is compatible with not having first-person authority about it, you cannot explain first-person authority either.

ND: I grant that your therapist might inform you that you are angry without your becoming consciously angry. If your knowledge that you are angry is based on *testimony,* then you aren't consciously angry and you won't speak with first-person authority about your anger.

What's needed in order to be consciously angry—what's needed for first-person authority—is *perceptual* self-knowledge. It isn't enough that you *somehow* find out that you're angry. Being consciously angry is like having a thing *in view,* not like learning something at second hand. When you are consciously angry, you can *track* changes in your anger as they occur. First-person authority is like the authority of an eyewitness. It can be explained if we say (as most new detectivists have) that the mechanism which enables us to detect our own mental states is a *perceptual* one.

AD: But a person might perceive that he's angry without being consciously angry. Imagine someone who can tell that he is angry by watching his own face in a mirror. (Maybe he's a genius at reading people's faces.) He might be able to track subtle changes in his anger this way, but if his self-awareness were based on what he saw in the mirror, he would not be consciously angry, and he would not speak about his anger with first-person authority.

It's precisely here that old detectivism was more appealing than new detectivism. The old detectivist said, "We know our own minds by inner sense," but what he meant by "inner sense" was something very different from seeing or hearing. At least such a view registered a kind of appreciation of the fact that being consciously angry is very different from being aware of objects and events that one sees or hears. (The problem with old detectivism was the *way* that it registered its appreciation of this difference—by representing our relation to inner states and events as involving a supernaturally reliable and direct kind of detection.) But you new detectivists try to explain consciousness by appealing to a cognitive mechanism that is on all fours with seeing and hearing. So against your kind of detectivism, the case of someone who looks in the mirror and sees that he's unconsciously angry may be adduced as a counterexample.

ND: I never claimed that just *any* sort of perception would suffice for consciousness. My position is that I am consciously angry when I perceive that I'm angry *in the right way*—let us say: via the operation of an *inner* sense. The word "consciously" indicates that a *particular* mode of perceptual access is in play.

AD: But you don't *explain* anything by so using the word "particular." You need to say what the relevant difference is between this inner sense and the outer senses. You need to make it intelligible that this inner sense, unlike any of the outer senses, gives rise to consciousness and first-person authority. I don't think you can. The importance of consciousness just isn't like the importance we attach to learning something by this, rather than that, mode of perception—by, for example, hearing rather than seeing. I might pay a therapist for years with the aim of bringing emotions to consciousness that I already know myself to harbor unconsciously, e.g., with the aim of becoming consciously angry at my parents or consciously sad about my violent childhood. Imagine someone who is almost never consciously angry, sad, lustful, proud, or jealous, but who is such a keen observer of his own behavior that he can say more about the unconscious occurrence of these emotions in himself than most people can say about the occurrence of these emotions (conscious or unconscious) in themselves. The life of such a person would be importantly incomplete: it would be thin, cold, and impoverished. The difference between a life impoverished in this way and a life of ordinary self-awareness cannot be understood as the difference between learning a set of facts by one mode of perception rather than another.

ND: I agree that a person who was never consciously sad or angry (etc.) would have a thin life. But my conception of self-knowledge as a mode of perception *is* able to do justice to the kind of incompleteness that would characterize such a life. A blind man suffers a related kind of incompleteness; he lacks a certain sort of phenomenology. Each mode of perception provides us with phenomenology as well as information. We *savor* moments of staring out over the ocean, hearing sea gulls call, smelling the sea breeze, etc. The inner sense is no exception; it provides us with a particular sort of phenomenology. This accounts for much of its importance in our lives.

AD: Imagine a person with blindsight across his entire visual field.[15] He would not savor moments of staring out over the ocean. Only *conscious* seeing involves the sort of phenomenology that you're talking about. I take it that given your other views, you ought to understand conscious seeing as: seeing plus perceiving that one is seeing via the inner sense. So really, it's not the case that on your view, each mode of perception provides its own distinctive phenomenology; only the inner sense provides us with phenomenology. Introducing the topic of phenomenology only makes your view more difficult to maintain. How can we understand the inner sense as just one among several senses given its *unique* connection to phenomenology?

15. Someone is said to suffer from blindsight if his primary visual cortex has been damaged in such a way that he retains the ability to visually detect features of stimuli in the affected region of his visual field even though he claims to be unable to see the stimuli. (So: the neurologist asks, "In which direction is the light moving?" whereupon the patient replies, "I can't see anything on that side of me." The neurologist then instructs the patient to just *guess* at the direction of movement, and the patient's guesses are correct.) Such people are often said to see the stimuli unconsciously. AD is imagining a person who has blindsight across his whole visual field. Actually, no such person has been documented, but this may be merely because no one has suffered the right sort of damage bilaterally.

Anyway, I don't think we should be talking about phenomenology. You yourself want to say that the inner sense discloses such mental states as believing, intending, and hoping. Yet, there isn't any characteristic phenomenology associated with consciously believing, intending, or hoping. Still, just as there is an important difference between my being consciously jealous and my knowing that I'm unconsciously jealous, there is an important difference between my consciously believing, for example, that my parents never wanted me, and my knowing that I believe this unconsciously.[16] You can go on saying that somehow, it's the mode of perception that makes the difference. But how? Once we've seen that what's at issue is not phenomenology, how can we think that the mere fact that I know my state by this, rather than that, mode of perception could matter so much to my life?

ND: Let me try another tack. Seeing a thing is different from being told about it—not just because I can track what I see and not just because of phenomenology, but because there is a kind of informational or aspectual richness that comes with seeing. When I'm describing an object that I have in view, I can go on and on about it. When I see, e.g., my dining room table, I see it *as* brown, *as* dirty, *as* round . . . (Moreover I see the brown *as* dark, *as* saturated . . .) There is no end of aspects here.

Each mode of perception comes with its own sort of aspectual richness. I see my guitar as shiny, reddish, unusually small; I hear it as slightly out of tune, warm, old-sounding; I feel it as cool, dry, and cracked. Perhaps what's important about the difference between learning that I'm jealous via the inner sense and learning this via some other sense lies in the aspectual richness associated with the inner sense.[17]

AD: Well, I *can* go on and on, both when I'm describing an object in my visual field and when I'm talking about my state of mind. I don't know that I could go on *endlessly* about my anger, but I can

---

16. A related point: there is nothing Moore-paradoxical about saying, "I unconsciously believe that my parents never wanted me, but actually, they wanted me quite a lot."

17. Lycan (1996) writes: "I must reemphasize my presumption that internal monitoring normally or often does give rise to introspective belief, and I should also note that, again on the model of external perception, introspection presents its object under an aspect, *as* being a certain way" (27).

usually say how extreme it is, at whom it is directed, and what it's about. But it is a mistake, nevertheless, to assimilate mental state avowals to descriptions of observed objects. To see why, notice first that my seeing an object as ϕ does not preclude my also hearing or feeling it as ϕ. I might both see and feel some object as, for example, cracked. If I understand what you mean by "aspects," bats and dolphins *hear* many of the aspects of things that we see. They hear things as large, curved, rough, off to the left, etc.[18]

Now given a new detectivist's conception of the mind, we should be able to imagine someone's *seeing* the very aspects of his own, say, anger that are, typically, inwardly sensed—someone who visually inspects his own brain (or face or behavior) and sees, e.g., that he is mildly angry at so-and-so for such-and-such. Consider a case in which someone is able to assert that he is mildly angry with his uncle only on the basis of some such visual feat. If what mattered about consciousness lay in a subject's inwardly perceiving aspects of his own inner state, then such a person would have what matters. He would be as good as consciously angry. But such a person would not be as good as consciously angry; he'd be utterly detached from his anger. Here's another example that brings out the same point: if I were able to talk about some belief of mine (including my degree of conviction and whatever other aspects I'm normally able to report) only thanks to a visual inspection of my brain or behavior, the belief would not be *mine* in the way that conscious beliefs are mine. If it became apparent to me that the belief was false, I would not be *surprised* in the way that a conscious believer is surprised when he finds that his belief is false. The significance of consciousness in our lives does not lie in the aspectual richness associated with some inner sense.

I'll sum up. In order for me to speak with first-person authority about one of my states of mind, it is not enough that I *know* of or about the state; it must be *conscious*. I might know a good deal about one of my unconscious states of mind; in such a circum-

18. If you're inclined to object that a bat or dolphin cannot hear anything as, e.g., curved because bats and dolphins lack concepts, then let the point concern an imagined creature who has both the concept *curved* and a capacity for echolocation.

stance, I would not speak about it with first-person authority. Objects of perception (or more broadly, detection)—e.g., the table before me—are said to be "known" rather than "conscious." (My seeing a table doesn't make it correct to say, "The table is conscious.") Therefore, merely positing an *inner* mechanism of perception (or detection) does not explain first-person authority. This is not to deny—nor, of course, is it to affirm—the existence of a mechanism by which we inwardly perceive our own states of mind. The point is that the discovery of such a mechanism wouldn't account for consciousness or first-person authority.

You have claimed that your postulated inner sense differs from the outer senses in that it makes its objects conscious and so makes them items about which we have first-person authority. You've failed, however, to explain *how* a mechanism of perception (or of detection) could have this power. In the absence of such an explanation, you simply have no account of either consciousness or first-person authority.

The shift from old to new detectivism could be compared to what happens in bad psychotherapy: the patient gives the appearance of improving while his neurotic defenses, which need to be broken down, are strengthened. The old detectivist's *problem* was that he understood a mental state's being conscious too much on the model of a table's being perceived—even if "inner sense" was taken to be radically different in nature from "outer sense." With the emergence of new detectivism, philosophers tried to avoid the twin pitfalls of dualism and scepticism by understanding the relations we bear to our own conscious mental states to be even *more* like those we bear to tables and chairs. I have argued that the result is a picture of mind that leaves first-person authority looking like a mystery.

If we reject detectivism, both old and new, how are we to make sense of first-person authority? In Chapter 2, I'll discuss what can appear to be the only answer to this question.

Constitutivism

What accounts for the special authority with which we speak about our own inner states and events? In Chapter 1, I tried to show that no form of detectivism is likely to yield a satisfactory answer to this question. In the present chapter, I'll discuss another approach toward making sense of first-person authority. According to this approach, there is no need for me to engage in anything like self-observation in order to state, for example, what I intend to do this evening, because when I judge that I intend to go to bed early, I thereby make it the case that this is what I intend. My authority concerning my own states of mind is not like the authority of an eyewitness. It might be better compared to that of an Army colonel when he *declares* an area off limits. The colonel needn't be better informed about the area than his soldiers are. His authority consists in the fact that what he says goes. According to what I'll be calling "constitutivism," my authority concerning my own states of mind comes to this: typically, what I say or think about my own mental state plays a constitutive role in determining what it is. Mental state self-ascriptions are unlike observation reports in that they constitute, to some significant extent, the facts to which they refer.

It might seem as if we must choose between some form of detectivism and some form of constitutivism when we try to account for first-person authority. ("Either I'm in a good position to discover my own mental states, or I don't so much discover as construct them.")[1] If one

1. Wright (2001b) asks us to consider the following biconditional: "X intends that P if and only if X is disposed to avow the intention that P, and would be sincere in so

is in this frame of mind—if one thinks that detectivism and constitutivism together exhaust the reasonable approaches toward understanding the authority with which we speak about own mental states—then it will be natural to read Wittgenstein, who often speaks against detectivism,[2] as some sort of constitutivist.

In the present chapter, I'll first discuss a reading of Wittgenstein suggested by Wright, one according to which Wittgenstein embraces a constitutivist account of first-person authority. (Wright himself is convinced by this account of first-person authority and thinks Wittgenstein *might* be as well. He is, however, hesitant about definitely ascribing it to him.) Later, I'll argue that neither this version of constitutivism nor any other will allow us to make good sense of first-person authority.

2.1. "A Kind of *Decision*"

The constitutivist position that Wright endorses and (hesitantly) ascribes to Wittgenstein is motivated in large part by a desire to make sense *not* of first-person authority, but of rule-following. Constitutivism more or less *follows* from lessons that Wright takes himself to find in Wittgenstein's discussions of rule-following. The present section has three parts. In what immediately follows, I shall introduce some of the material from the *Investigations* out of which Wright's argument for constitutivism emerges. Next, I'll say a little bit about Saul Kripke's enormously influential reading of the rule-following problematic. This is necessary because Wright presents *his* reading of Wittgenstein as an alternative to Kripke's (indeed, as providing an answer to the sceptic

doing, and fully grasps the content of that intention, and is prey to no material self-deception, and . . . and so on" (139). He goes on: "Now, such a biconditional may be read in two contrasting ways. One reading—the *detective*—would hold that the left-hand side serves to describe a determinate state of affairs which, if all the provisos on the right-hand side are met, the subject is able to *apprehend*. On this view, the provisos collectively determine the conditions for a cognitive success, which an avowal may then serve to report. The alternative, however, is to accord priority to the right-hand side. The resulting view would see the disposition to make the avowal as *constituting* the state of affairs reported by the left-hand side when the provisos are met" (139–140). If we accord priority to the right-hand side of the biconditional, we get what Wright calls the "constitutive reading" of it. (I settled on the terms "detectivism" and "constitutivism" after reading this paper of Wright's.)

2. See the Introduction.

who figures as a character in Kripke's text). Finally, I'll come to what Wright himself has to say about Wittgenstein on rule-following and first-person authority.

*   *   *

A rule (or an order or an instruction) seems to provide a standard against which a person trying to follow it may be judged—as either behaving in accord with it or not. A central concern of Wittgenstein's later work is how we are to understand this notion of accord. At *PI* §185ff., Wittgenstein asks us to imagine a pupil who has been taught to write out various mathematical series when given instructions of the form "+n." His teacher says, "+2," and he writes, "2, 4, 6," etc. But when the pupil is asked to continue the +2 series beyond 1000, he writes, "998, 1000, 1004, 1008." Two questions arise: First, how is the pupil supposed to know what the order calls for him to do after he has written "1000"? (He has not been *explicitly* trained to write "1002" immediately after "1000.") And second, what determines that "1002" is in fact what he's supposed to write at that point; what fixes it that writing "1002" after "1000" would accord with the teacher's instruction?

One kind of answer to these questions would appeal to the notion of interpretation. We might say that what determines that the teacher's utterance—"+2"—calls for the pupil to write "1002" immediately after "1000" is that the teacher attaches a particular interpretation to it. We might say, moreover, that the pupil's understanding the utterance requires that he attach the same, or a suitably similar, interpretation to it. But here we run into a problem. For let us allow that the teacher and the pupil *do* attach an interpretation—the same interpretation—to what the teacher says. Let's say that they both take "+2" to mean: *Write "2, 4, 6," and just continue to write the next but one number after every number that you've written.* How is the pupil to know that *this* sentence requires him to write "1002" after "1000"? And what determines that this sentence does indeed call for "1002" to be written at that point?

If we say that what a rule requires or means is determined by its interpretation, we are left wondering how the interpretation gets *its* meaning. If we say that the interpretation requires its *own* interpretation, an infinite regress threatens: each interpretation that we introduce requires the support of another. Thus at *PI* §198, Wittgenstein writes:

[A]ny interpretation still hangs in the air along with what it interprets, and cannot give it any support. Interpretations by themselves do not determine meaning.

This conclusion gives rise to the famous paradox of *PI* §201:

> This was our paradox: no course of action could be determined by a rule, because every course of action can be made out to accord with the rule. The answer was: if everything can be made out to accord with the rule, then it can also be made out to conflict with it. And so there would be neither accord nor conflict here.

As we'll see, Wright is concerned to avoid the paradox mentioned here without falling into *platonism*. We can think of platonism as an attempt to block the infinite regress of interpretations that gives rise to the paradox by positing special items that—unlike noises, marks, and gestures—are, as it were, intrinsically significant: they neither need nor brook interpretation. According to the platonist, what saves our words from emptiness is that such items stand behind them. The regress of interpretations does not arise as a problem because these intrinsically significant items neither need be, nor can be, interpreted. We should read Wittgenstein as describing the impulse toward such a position when he writes:

> What one wishes to say is: "Every sign is capable of interpretation; but the *meaning* mustn't be capable of interpretation. It is the last interpretation." (*B&B*, 34)

I want to mention two reasons why we ought to be dissatisfied with a platonistic account of meaning and understanding. Here's one: if we say that all of our words and gestures derive their semantic significance from items that lie hidden behind them, then communication comes to look deeply mysterious. How is it that when I say something to you, you not only hear my words but you generally grasp my meaning? A platonist might say: "My words and gestures can be interpreted any which way, but the thing behind them, the meaning, needs no interpretation. Now, I can't convey this item directly to my interlocutor. All that I can do is talk to him, or gesture to him, and all my words and gestures can be interpreted in various ways. But if he's lucky, he'll guess what I have in mind and understand me."[3] On this picture of things, if you and I are to succeed in communicating, we must be fortunate enough to guess each other's meanings correctly. Not only must we correctly guess the meanings of each other's words; there is no way for us to determine that any of our guesses have been correct. You can't tell me whether I have guessed your meaning correctly because you can only guess at what I have guessed. Given this picture of communication, a *conversation* might be modeled by the following game: You draw a picture on a piece of paper that I am not allowed to look at. Although I cannot see your drawing, I now try to produce a copy of it on a piece of paper that *you* cannot see. We go back and forth like this without ever showing each other our drawings.[4]

I said that I would mention two problems with platonism—with the picture of meaning as "the last interpretation." One of these is that platonism makes communication look like a miracle. Another is that the platonist really has no idea how anything *could* block the regress of interpretations and so be "the last interpretation"—no idea how something could be a fount from which our dead noises and marks derive their significance, rather than just another intrinsically contentless item awaiting interpretation. The platonist is driven in the course of his theorizing to say that there are, there *must* be, such items (else our words would be mere empty noises and marks), but these items seem mysterious even to him.

*   *   *

3. Wittgenstein depicts the platonist's sense that communication requires guessing in passages such as the following: "But do you really explain to the other person what you yourself understand? Don't you get him to *guess* the essential thing? You give examples,—but he has to guess their drift . . ." (*PI* §210). And: "Once he has seen the right thing, seen the one of infinitely many references which I am trying to push him towards—once he has got hold of it, he will continue the series right without further ado. I grant that he can only guess (intuitively guess) the reference that I mean—but once he has managed that the game is won" (*Z* §304).

4. Compare the game just described with a well-known example that Wittgenstein presents in the context of a discussion of pain: "Suppose everyone had a box with something in it: we call it a 'beetle.' No one can look into anyone else's box, and everyone says he knows what a beetle is only by looking at *his* beetle" (*PI* §293). I would argue that, according to Wittgenstein, the same philosophical pressures that underlie the platonist's view of meaning also underlie a picture in which thoughts and feelings appear mind-bogglingly private. (See §4.2 for a discussion of almost this point.)

According to Kripke, what's at issue in Wittgenstein's discussions of rule-following is a form of scepticism according to which there are no facts concerning what our words mean. Kripke tries to illustrate the line of thought that leads to this remarkable conclusion by asking us to imagine a sceptic who challenges his interlocutor to show that, given what he had always meant by the term "plus" in the past, the correct answer to the question "What is 68 plus 57?" is "125" rather than "5." In other words, the sceptic challenges his interlocutor to prove that in the past he'd meant *plus* by "plus" rather than some function (the "quus" function) whose value is 5 when its arguments are 68 and 57. The interlocutor is to meet this challenge by citing facts about his own past life that his meaning *plus* by "plus" had consisted in. A range of facts are adduced—facts not only about how the interlocutor has interpreted the word "plus," but also about the circumstances under which he's used it, about his dispositions to use it, and about occurrent mental episodes he's undergone in connection with it. The sceptic argues persuasively that none of these could have determined, for an infinity of possible applications of "plus," which ones would accord with what the interlocutor had meant by the word. The sceptic concludes that there is no fact about what his interlocutor had meant by "plus." From here, he argues that there are, in general, no facts about what our signs mean.

The problem raised by Kripke's sceptic threatens more than the idea that there are facts about what we mean when we speak and write. It is as much a problem about how there could be contentful *mental* phenomena. Kripke's sceptic might have challenged his interlocutor to show that he'd ever had an *intention* to add (rather than to "quadd") with similar results. (Indeed, Kripke sometimes puts the point this way.) Just as a person's having meant something determinate by the word "plus" requires that there be facts about whether an infinity of possible uses of it would accord with what she meant, someone's having had a determinate intention (or desire or wish) requires that there be facts about whether an infinity of possible states of affairs would accord with what she'd intended (or desired or wished). The conclusion reached by Kripke's sceptic amounts to the claim that there are no content-facts at all, and so no facts about what someone intends or wishes, any more than facts about what she means when she speaks.

According to Kripke, Wittgenstein recommends a "sceptical solution" to the problem that is posed by the sceptic, i.e., a response to scepticism which concedes "that the sceptic's negative assertions are unanswerable" (Kripke 1982, 66). Precisely *which* negative assertions does Kripke take Wittgenstein to concede to the sceptic? Because Kripke's text invites more than one answer to this question, I find it difficult to get into clear focus the sceptical solution that he means to attribute to Wittgenstein.[5] There is, however, a prevailing interpretation of Kripke's Wittgenstein, and, for present purposes, it will suffice for me to summarize it. According to this interpretation, Kripke's Wittgenstein concedes to the sceptic that a sentence like "Jones means *plus* by 'plus'" (or "Jones intends to add") cannot be used to state a fact because there is nothing about Jones's behavior or state of mind for such a fact to consist in. What saves assertions about meaning from being pointless is that such talk may be used for purposes other than that of stating facts.[6] While a sentence like "Jones means *plus*" cannot be true, it may yet have a kind of correctness: its utterance may be justi-

5. On the one hand, Kripke says that although Wittgenstein might resist admitting it in so many words, he concedes to the sceptic that there are no facts of the matter concerning what we mean: "Wittgenstein, perhaps cagily, might well disapprove of the straightforward formulation [of his response to scepticism] given here. Nevertheless I choose to be so bold as to say: Wittgenstein holds, with the sceptic, that there is no fact as to whether I mean plus or quus" (Kripke 1982, 70–71). On the other hand, Kripke ascribes a deflationist view of facts to Wittgenstein: "Like many others, Wittgenstein accepts the 'redundancy' theory of truth: to affirm that a statement is true (or presumably, to precede it with 'It is a fact that . . .') is simply to affirm the statement itself, and to say it is not true is to deny it: ($'p'$ is true $= p$)" (1982, 86). Moreover, he suggests that Wittgenstein would not "wish to deny the propriety of an ordinary use of the phrase 'the fact that Jones meant addition by such-and-such symbol'" (1982, 69). There is a tension between these two strands in Kripke's reading of Wittgenstein—a tension that makes it hard to see just what the "sceptical solution" is supposed to come to.

6. Wright understands Kripke in this way. He writes: "According to Kripke's Wittgenstein, all our discourse concerning meaning, understanding, content, and cognate notions, fails of strict factuality—says nothing literally true or false—and is saved from vacuity only by a 'Sceptical Solution,' a set of proposals for rehabilitating meaning-talk in ways that prescind from the assignment to it of any fact-stating role" (Wright 2001e, 172). For other readings of Kripke that more or less agree with this characterization of the sceptical solution, see, e.g., Baker and Hacker 1984, 4; Boghossian 1989, 518; and McDowell 1998c, 266. I'm familiar with two commentators who argue that, contrary to the received reading of Kripke, Kripke's Wittgenstein does not concede that attributions of meaning must be non-factual. These are Byrne (1996) and Wilson (1998).

fied within a communal language-game. Such a sentence may be used to register our acceptance of Jones into the linguistic community. We, as it were, pin a membership badge on him when we say, "He means *plus* by 'plus'"; we accept him as one of us.

*   *   *

At least as he is widely understood, then, Kripke takes the central conclusion of Wittgenstein's *Investigations* to be that there can be no fact of the matter concerning what it is that someone means, intends, or wishes. Now, Wright rejects this conclusion; moreover, he rejects the reading of the *Investigations* according to which Wittgenstein endorses it. Wright follows a number of other commentators[7] in noting that Kripke's sceptic unjustifiably assumes that if there are facts about content, they must reduce to facts that can be characterized in terms of contentless states and events:

> [T]here is an explicit and unacceptable reductionism involved at the stage at which the Sceptic challenges his interlocutor to recall some aspect of his former mental life which might constitute his, for example, having meant addition by 'plus.' It is not acceptable, apparently, if the interlocutor claims to recall precisely that.   (Wright 2001e, 176; see also 2001a, especially 147)

According to Wright, the correct answer to the challenge raised by Kripke's sceptic is what he calls a "flat-footed response" (Wright 2001e, 177) along the following lines: *The fact about my past usage of "plus" that fixes it that I am now acting in accord with what I then meant by "plus" is just that I meant* plus *by "plus."* Wright thinks, moreover, that Wittgenstein would have endorsed such a response. But, he says, this leaves us with a real problem, that "of seeing how and why the correct answer just given can *be* correct" (2001e, 177).

Wright begins his explanation of how and why the flat-footed response to Kripke's sceptic can be correct by describing a temptation that, he points out, Wittgenstein is concerned to undermine—the temptation to think that when I give someone a rule to follow, e.g., a rule governing an arithmetical series, I must somehow bring him to guess what I have in mind. I might say, "Continue the series that begins

7. See, e.g., McDowell 1998f; McGinn 1984; and Goldfarb 1985.

2, 4, 6, 8, 10." Or I might say, "Start with 2 and just keep adding 2." But I can't name *all* the numbers in the series, and *whatever* words I say to my interlocutor, they will be amenable to various interpretations—e.g., interpretations under which the series that I have in mind includes a segment that goes: 1000, 1004. So we are tempted to think that my interlocutor's coming to understand me aright requires that he guess at the essential thing *behind* my words—my meaning or intention—where this is understood to transcend any description or explanation that I can give of it. We are tempted, Wright says, toward platonism.

What does Wright think we should say about rule-following if we are not satisfied with platonism? He puts what he takes to be one of the central lessons of Wittgenstein's discussions of rule-following as follows: "*It might be preferable, in describing our most basic rule-governed responses, to think of them as informed not by an* intuition *(of the requirements of the rule) but a kind of* decision" (2001e, 182). The platonist thinks that a rule (or anyway, the meaning that lies behind the statement of a rule) autonomously calls for a course of action and that when we set out to follow a rule, we intuit, or perceive, what it requires us to do. According to Wright's Wittgenstein, this sort of platonism should be rejected: when we follow rules, we don't perceive their requirements; we *decide* them.

A problem with saying that we decide a rule's requirements is that this suggests a rule-follower is free to decide that anything she happens to do is what the rule calls for. Wright is aware of this problem, describing it as follows:

> The rule-following considerations attack the idea that judgments about the requirements of a rule on a particular occasion have a 'tracking' epistemology, answer to states of affairs constituted altogether independently of our inclination to make those judgments. How can judgments lack a substantial epistemology in this way, and yet still be *objective*—still have to answer to something distinct from our actual dispositions of judgment? (2001e, 191)

Wright's answer to the question raised in this passage is to say that it is only our "best" judgments (i.e., our best *decisions*) about the statement of a rule that determine what it means or requires—where a judgment is a *best* judgment if it is arrived at under certain ideal conditions, which Wright calls "C-conditions." Judgments made about rules are objective by virtue of the fact that when the C-conditions are *not* satisfied, such judgments are constrained by the characteristics of rules that are determined by C-conditioned judgments.[8] Thus Wright, taking himself to be following Wittgenstein, claims that what a rule requires is decided by our best judgments or opinions about the matter.

* * *

Just as what I do in my kitchen may accord or fail to accord with a rule—a recipe—printed in a book, it may accord or not with one of my wishes, intentions, or fears (e.g., my intention to bake a prize-winning rhubarb pie or my fear that I'll set off the smoke detector). Such mental states are liable to give rise to the same philosophical disquietude that rules engender.[9] Wright thinks we should reject the idea that an intention somehow autonomously picks out the activities that would accord with it and instead accept that our best judgments determine whether or not some activity counts as the carrying out of an intention. The lesson he draws from Wittgenstein's writing is that the content of an intentional state, like that of a rule, is a matter for us to decide.

Now, as we have seen, Wright relies on the notion of a "best" judgment or opinion, one arrived at under C-conditions, in order to confer a kind of objectivity upon rules and intentional states. Exactly what conditions does he have in mind? Although he is less forthcoming about this than we might have hoped, Wright does say that under most *ordinary* conditions, if I make a judgment about what I myself intend or intended, wish or wished, mean or meant, etc., it is a best judgment. This is to say, for judgments or opinions that may be expressed in the form of avowals of meaning, intention, desire, etc., the C-conditions are usually satisfied. Typically, according to Wright, when I judge that I

8. See Wright 2001e, 195, n. 36.

9. Thus, Wittgenstein writes: "If I try to describe the process of intention, I feel first and foremost that it can do what it is supposed to only by containing an extremely faithful picture of what it intends. But further, that that too does not go far enough, because a picture, whatever it may be, can be variously interpreted; hence this picture too in its turn stands isolated. When one has the picture in view by itself it is suddenly dead, and it is as if something had been taken away from it, which had given it life before. It is not a thought, not an intention; whatever accompaniments we imagine for it, articulate or inarticulate processes, or any feeling whatsoever, it remains isolated, it does not point outside itself to a reality beyond" (*Z* §236).

intended to do X, I make it the case that X was what I intended to do.[10] Thus Wright ends up with a constitutivist account of first-person authority:

> [W]hy is it *a priori* reasonable to believe that, provided Jones has the relevant concepts and is attentive to the matter, he will believe that he intends to ϕ if and only if he does? . . . [T]he matter will be nicely explained if the concept of intention works in such a way that Jones's opinions, formed under the restricted set of C-conditions, play [an] extension-determining role. (2001e, 203)[11]

Jones is generally right about his own intentions (or wishes or desires) because, under ordinary conditions, his taking himself to have a particular intention fixes it that he does.[12]

Recall that in Kripke's discussion of Wittgenstein, a sceptic asks his interlocutor, "What is 68 plus 57?" The interlocutor answers, "125," whereupon the sceptic suggests that, given what the interlocutor had always meant by "plus" in the past, the correct answer is "5." The scep-

10. Wright notes that this determination is defeasible. What a subject says about his own intentional states is generally allowed to stand, but subsequent events occasionally overturn his judgment.

11. About the expression "extension-determining," Wright says: "The contrast . . . is between judgments among which our best opinions *determine* the extension of the truth-predicate, and those among which they at most reflect an extension determined independently" (2001e, 192).

12. We might wonder: Is it a subject's publicly *declaring* that he intends a particular thing that constitutes his so intending, or is it sufficient for him merely to be of the opinion that he intends it? In Wright 2001c, the emphasis is on opinions or decisions. In an earlier paper, Wright focuses a bit more on a subject's declarations concerning his own intentions. There, he writes: "The authority which our self-ascriptions of meaning, intention, and decision assume is not based on any kind of cognitive advantage, expertise or achievement. Rather it is, as it were, a *concession,* unofficially granted to anyone whom one takes seriously as a rational subject. It is, so to speak, such a subject's right to declare what he intends, what he intended, and what satisfies his intentions; and his possession of this right consists in the conferral upon such declarations, other things being equal, of a *constitutive* rather than descriptive role" (2001b, 137–138). On such a view, a subject's authority about his own intentions is *very much* like the authority of an army colonel when he declares an area off-limits. In §2.3, I will distinguish between "avowal-constitutivism," according to which avowals are what constitute our intentions, and "belief-constitutivism," according to which mere judgments or beliefs do the constitutive work. Nothing in my criticism of Wright's view will hang on which of these positions we take him to be recommending.

tic challenges his interlocutor to say in what the fact that he had previously meant *plus* by "plus" might have consisted. When the interlocutor fails to provide an answer that can satisfy the sceptic, the latter concludes that there is no fact of the matter concerning what his interlocutor meant. Earlier, I noted that Wright endorses a flat-footed answer to Kripke's sceptic—one that goes: *The fact about my past usage of "plus" that fixes it that I am now acting in accord with what I then meant by "plus" is just that I meant* plus *by "plus."* I also noted that Wright wants to provide an explanation of *how* such an answer could be the correct one. We're now in a position to consider Wright's explanation:

> It will be . . . a perfect answer to Kripke's Sceptic to explain how judgments concerning one's own meanings, both past and present, are . . . provisionally extension-determining in the most ordinary circumstances. Challenged to justify the claim that I formerly meant addition by 'plus,' it will not be necessary to locate some meaning-constitutive fact in my former behaviour or mental life. A sufficient answer need only advert to my present opinion, that addition is what I formerly meant, and still mean, and to the *a priori* reasonableness of the supposition, failing evidence to the contrary, that this opinion is best. (Wright 2001e, 206)

Kripke's sceptic challenges his interlocutor to cite some fact or facts *about his former life* that his meaning *plus* by "plus" consisted in. The sceptic presupposes that if his interlocutor meant anything determinate in the past by "plus," there must be such facts. Wright rejects this presupposition. On his view, what someone meant in the past can be constituted by judgments he makes in the present. According to Wright, when I answer the sceptic in the flat-footed fashion—when I issue the avowal "I meant *plus* by 'plus'"—I *make* it the case that I meant *plus* by "plus." We could say that I make it the case that the rule I have always attached to the word "plus" calls for me to answer, "125," rather than, "5," in response to the question "What is 68 plus 57?"

Ordinarily, when someone makes it the case that a stated rule calls for one activity rather than another, we describe him as stipulating what the rule requires. Imagine, for example, that a pamphlet entitled *Rules for Students* is issued to seventh-graders on the first day of school. The pamphlet includes the following sentence: "While in class, students shall conduct themselves in an orderly fashion." A teacher might stipulate that, in his classroom, following this rule requires that students sit in alphabetical order. We might characterize Wright as claiming that every rule and every intentional state gets its content by a kind of stipulation. My aim in the next section will be to bring out what is wrong both with this position, which I'll sometimes call "stipulativism," and with the kind of constitutivism to which it gives rise. Before I turn to this task, however, I need to say a bit more about the *Investigations* and the way in which the problem that Wright takes himself to be addressing is set up there.

2.2. Interpretation and Stipulation

> It is wrong to say: I meant him by looking at him. "Meaning" does not stand for an activity which wholly or partly consists in the expressions of meaning.   (*Z* §19)

At *PI* §431, Wittgenstein has an interlocutor say:

> "There is a gulf between an order and its execution. It has to be filled by the act of understanding."

In saying that there's "a gulf between an order and its execution," Wittgenstein's interlocutor means that a sequence of written or spoken words cannot be understood without some "act" to serve as a bridge between the words themselves and what they mean. What sort of act could perform this function? Imagine that an American who speaks little Italian is traveling in Rome. A local police officer approaches her in the street and shouts something at her. The policeman's tone of voice and his facial expression suggest that he is issuing an order—as indeed he is—but our traveler can't make out *what* he wants her to do. Here, it would be natural to say that there was a gulf between the policeman's saying what he did and the traveler's understanding him. It would be equally natural to say that if the traveler managed to interpret the policeman's order into English (perhaps with the aid of a dictionary), the gulf would be bridged. So it seems that an act of *interpretation* can bridge the gulf between an order and its execution.

This conclusion, however, begins to wobble under the weight of the following line of thought: "We need not imagine the meeting of different languages (such as English and Italian) if all that we want is an example of a case in which there's a gulf between an order and its execution. There's a gulf between *any* order and its execution. Any order could, conceivably, be misunderstood. Imagine that someone approaches you and says, 'Hands up!' He wants you to put your hands above your head, but you *might* misunderstand him; you might think, for example, that he wants you to turn your hands palms up directly in front of you. There's a gulf between even this simple an order and its execution: unless you interpret it properly, you won't know how to execute it as it was intended." This line of thought may sound innocuous, but it leads to a problem. Once we have come to think that there is a gulf between *any* order and its execution, interpretation no longer looks like a way to bridge such a gulf. Any interpretation that I attach to "Hands up!" will, itself, be such that it *could* be misunderstood. *It* will seem to stand in as much need of interpretation as "Hands up!" It will, as it were, come with its *own* gulf.[13] Once we take there to be a gulf between every order and its execution, we can't seem to find anything to bridge the gulfs.

The apparently innocuous thought—that there is a gulf between every order and its execution—might be argued for in a slightly different way. Someone might say: "An order, recipe, or instruction is, in itself, nothing but sounds or ink marks. Interpretation, or something like interpretation—some 'act of understanding'—is needed if the sounds or ink marks are to strike anyone as more than empty noises or squiggles. This goes for *any* order, recipe, or rule; there is a gap between any such item and what it requires." A thought like this is expressed in the second paragraph of *PI* §431. (I began this section by quoting its first paragraph.) Wittgenstein's interlocutor says:

13. Compare *PI* §433: "When we give an order, it can look as if the ultimate thing sought by the order had to remain unexpressed, as there is always a gulf between an order and its execution. Say I want someone to make a particular movement, say to raise his arm. To make it quite clear, I do the movement. This picture seems unambiguous till we ask: how does he know that *he is to make that movement*?—How does he know at all what use he is to make of the signs I give him, whatever they are?—Perhaps I shall now try to supplement the order by means of further signs, by pointing from myself to him, making encouraging gestures, etc. Here it looks as if the order were beginning to stammer."

"Only in the act of understanding is it meant that we are to do THIS. The *order*—why, that is nothing but sounds, ink-marks.—"

When we consider an order as mere ink marks, it seems dead, inert. It seems to us that a bridge is needed to link it with any determinate set of requirements. Interpretation is an obvious candidate to play the role of bridge, but—under the pressure of an insistence that there's a gulf between *any* string of words and what they mean—every interpretation seems inert as well.

The paradox of *PI* §201 has its roots in the thought that there is always a gulf between the statement of a rule—a string of words—and the rule's execution or application. Let's look again at the first paragraph of §201:

> This was our paradox: no course of action could be determined by a rule, because every course of action can be made out to accord with the rule. The answer was: if everything can be made out to accord with the rule, then it can also be made out to conflict with it. And so there would be neither accord nor conflict here.

In what sense *can* every course of action be made out to accord with a rule? Imagine that a line in a recipe book reads, "Beat six egg whites until stiff peaks form." If, in trying to follow this instruction, I were to beat six egg *yolks*, how could my action be made out to accord with the recipe? The paradox comes into view under the illumination of a thought like this: "The words 'Beat six egg whites' are just ink marks in a book. They call for one activity rather than another only on a particular interpretation, and ink marks can be interpreted *any* which way." Once we are in the grip of such a thought, we cannot escape the conclusion that "any interpretation still hangs in the air along with what it interprets, and cannot give it any support" (*PI* §198).

In Chapter 4, I'll argue that Wittgenstein's response to the paradox of §201 is to question the thought that there is a gulf between every rule and what it requires. For now, notice that this is not the course that Wright recommends. Wright suggests, in effect, that an appeal to (something like) stipulation can solve the problem that we had hoped to address by appealing to interpretation; he argues that even though interpretation cannot bridge the gulf between a rule and its application, stipulation can.

The thought that there is a gulf between every order and its execution has an analogue when we consider intentional states. An order is, typically, the spoken or written expression of someone's desire. If we have been moved to think that there is a gulf between every rule and what it requires, we will also think that there is a gulf between any human behavior and its psychological significance. It will seem to us that what we perceive when we look at another person are bodily movements and their effects (including sounds made by speaking), and that some sort of interpretation of these movements and effects is needed if we are to learn about the other person's intentions, wishes, hopes, etc. This view gives rise to a problem: any such interpretation will seem to stand in need of another interpretation, and *it* will stand in need of yet another, *ad infinitum*. Wright's solution to the problem is that intentional state attributions are not based on interpretation but on (what I've been calling) stipulation. I get to decide what it is that I have been intending, desiring, hoping, etc.

*   *   *

How might stipulation bridge a gulf between a rule and what it requires? Recall the example in which a pamphlet of rules for students has a line reading, "While in class, students shall conduct themselves in an orderly fashion." A teacher decides that this rule calls for his students to sit in alphabetical order. We might say that by stipulating what the rule requires, the teacher bridges a gulf between the rule, as it appears in the pamphlet, and its application in his classroom. As it appears in the pamphlet, the rule is imprecise. With his stipulation, the teacher clarifies what sort of behavior would accord with it, at least in his classroom. Does it make sense to suggest that this is how rules and intentional states quite generally acquire their content? Can stipulation play the role that interpretation cannot?

No. Once we are in the grip of the thought that there is a gulf between every rule and its application, stipulation looks as powerless as interpretation to bridge such a gulf. Any stipulation (whether we understand a stipulation to be a decision or opinion rendered in words or one that is, as it were, merely mental) will seem to us to "hang in the air" unless *it* is interpreted (or until a *further* stipulation is made). We've already seen where this goes: we wind up with a vicious regress. Wright thinks that our best *opinions* about the requirements of a rule (rather than our interpretations of it) determine what would accord with it. The problem with this view is that every opinion seems to stand in need of interpretation or stipulation, and any such interpretation or stipulation seems to stand in need of further interpretation or stipulation, *ad infinitum.* Thus, Wright's view is subject to the same objection as the view that interpretations determine the requirements of rules.

In order to accept a position like Wright's, we'd have to think that stipulations are regress-stoppers—that although rules, orders, and intentions, in themselves, have no content, stipulations *do.* We'd have to think that while an order stands in need of a stipulation if it is to be meaningful, a stipulation requires nothing outside itself. On such a view, stipulations are self-standing sources of significance—items that stand to the significance of rules and intentions as the sun stands to the light of the moon. The view amounts to a (nonstandard) form of platonism. According to this sort of platonism, although rules, intentions, recipes, and wishes are, in themselves, empty, stipulations are somehow intrinsically contentful.

I have been criticizing Wright's stipulativism—his view that all content derives from something like decision or stipulation. Let us now focus more narrowly on his constitutivism. According to Wright, first-person authority is due to the fact that each person decides the contents of her own mind when she judges what she intends or intended, desires or desired. This position suffers from the same problem as the more generic stipulativism about content. Once we've been gripped by the "paradox" of *PI* §201, these judgments (whether conceived of as mental or as spoken) seem, in themselves, contentless and thus to stand in need of interpretations (which, in turn, stand in need of further interpretations, *ad infinitum*). The point may be put as follows: Wright sees a gulf between the behavior of a human being, considered apart from judgments made about her, and its psychological significance. Her behavior is always subject to many widely divergent interpretations. Wright claims that our best opinions about a person's intentional states—often expressed in avowals—bridge this gulf. But once we are in the thrall of this picture of the relation between the inner and the outer, neither avowals nor the opinions that they express seem to be unproblematically contentful. Thus, they can be of no use in bridging a gulf between behavior and psychology.

2.3. The Responsibility Objection

As we have seen, Wright's constitutivism arises out of very broad considerations about the nature of meaning and understanding. I have argued against his version of constitutivism by trying to bring out what is wrong with his stipulativism—his view about content in general. But someone might be drawn to constitutivism as a way of accounting for first-person authority without committing himself to anything like Wright's position on content in general. Imagine a constitutivist who replies to my critique of Wright as follows: "I don't claim that our words or judgments derive their significance from interpretations or stipulations. I'm not putting forward any general theory of content, and I'm happy to grant that stipulativism is hopeless. It doesn't follow from this that I cannot explain first-person authority by way of the claim that our mental states are often constituted or determined by our self-ascriptions of them." In what remains of this chapter, I'll try to answer this interlocutor; I'll argue that constitutivism of any sort is a bad idea.

Let us distinguish four types of constitutivism according to the way in which a proponent would answer the following two questions: (1) *Is it a subject's publicly and sincerely avowing that he is in a particular state of mind that constitutes his being in it, or does it suffice for him merely to believe that he is in it?* I'll call someone who holds that public avowals are what do the, as it were, constitutive work an "avowal-constitutivist." I'll use the expression "belief-constitutivist" for someone who thinks that beliefs or judgments do this work. (2) *Which facts about our mental lives are fixed by self-ascriptions?* We seem to speak with special authority not only about our attitudes—beliefs, desires, intentions, etc.—but also about our sensations, passing thoughts, and mental images. In what follows, I'll distinguish between a constitutivist who seeks to account for the authority with which we speak about all these phenomena from one who concerns himself only with the self-ascription of attitudes.

Wright's constitutivism extends only to attitudes. Ideally, however, we'd like to understand the authority with which we speak about everything from beliefs to headaches. For this reason, I want to begin by considering a version of constitutivism that includes among its explananda the authority with which we speak about our own sensations.

More specifically, let us start with a version of constitutivism according to which I speak with authority about, e.g., my headaches because when I avow that I have one, I make it the case that I do.

A way to put what is wrong with such a position is that it doesn't leave enough room for sympathy. This kind of constitutivism represents my headache as the product of my describing myself, and self-describing is the sort of activity for which people are held responsible.[14] If my headache were constituted to any significant extent by my avowal, it would make sense to blame me for it. Now it does *sometimes* make sense to blame a person for having a headache, e.g., in a case where her headache is the result of her choosing to stay at a party until four in the morning. But this kind of case stands in marked contrast to one in which someone is born with a disposition to get migraines and without doing anything counter-indicated—without eating cheese or drinking red wine—she gets one. The sort of constitutivism we are considering asks us, in effect, to forget how to draw lines between cases in which compassion, consolation, and pity are appropriate and those in which they are not. A position according to which the migraine sufferer is to blame for her headaches is patently unattractive. (Moreover, even the late-night party goer, who *is* at least partly to blame for her headache, is not to blame *because she avows that she is in pain.*) Call this "the responsibility objection."

As stated, the responsibility objection speaks against only a quite specific type of constitutivism—one according to which sensation avowals make themselves true—and this type does not have a great deal of *prima facie* plausibility. I'll be trying to show that other sorts of constitutivism are susceptible to alternative formulations of the same objection. For this reason, I'm going to let the dialectic play itself out a little more. I'll ask you to consider two replies to the responsibility objection on behalf of avowal-constitutivism about sensations:

Reply 1: "As our knowledge of the world increases, what we are responsible for changes. Suppose I learn that a term I've been using to refer to people from Newfoundland has insulting connotations. My accountability changes. I become responsible for the hurt feelings I cause by continuing to use the term. Most migraine sufferers are not

14. There are ways of describing oneself that are, e.g., insensitive to the feelings of others. ("At least I sing better than you people do.")

now responsible for their pain, but if they were to learn that their headaches were constituted by their self-descriptions, they would become responsible."

According to this reply, people who complain of migraines deserve our compassion—but only until they learn the truth of constitutivism. What goes missing here is an acknowledgment of the fact that what's awful about headaches is not the avowing of them; it's the headaches themselves.

Reply 2: "Isn't it possible that we should discover that we bring about, or make worse, our headaches by talking about them? Are you ruling this out a priori?"

I'm not ruling this out. We might discover that saying, "I have a migraine" is like drinking red wine or eating cheese. But the constitutivist about pains isn't claiming to have made such a discovery. His point is not that I cause my headache by saying "I have a migraine." He believes that my saying "I have a headache" constitutes my having one. And we've seen that *this* claim should be rejected.

Avowal-constitutivism cannot explain the authority with which we speak about our own sensations. Let us now consider a version of constitutivism according to which we constitute our sensations not by avowing them, but by believing ourselves to have them. A proponent of this sort of position might respond to the last few paragraphs as follows: "The problem with avowal-constitutivism is that avowals are actions. A person is responsible for his avowals in ways that he is not responsible for his states of mind. On my view—'belief-constitutivism'—what fixes it that a person, e.g., has a headache is that she believes herself to have one. I'm not claiming that we 'decide our pains' (we don't, after all, decide our beliefs), so you can't accuse me of overextending the space of our responsibility."

The problem with shifting from avowals to beliefs in this way is that there *is* a kind of responsibility that we bear for our beliefs but that we don't bear for our sensations. Imagine that you have the following conversation with the belief-constitutivist:

> *Belief-constitutivist:* I have a terrible headache.
> *You:* Do you have any idea what brought it on?
> *B-c:* Oh, you know; I started believing that I had a headache, and that fixed it that I did.

You: But *why* did you start believing that you had a headache? Did you just decide to start believing that?

What answer could the belief-constitutivist give you? He might say something like this: "I didn't just *decide* to believe that I had a headache. I was exposed to a number of stresses and loud noises, after which I couldn't help but believe that I had one. The stressful stimuli caused me to believe I had a headache, and the belief constituted its own truth."

Here, the belief-constitutivist tries to do justice to the fact that he is passive in the face of his headaches by claiming that stressful events cause him to believe that he has them. He says, "After I've been exposed to certain environmental stresses, I *can't help but* believe that I have a headache." But there is a problem with this use of "can't help but." Compare the following uses of this phrase: (a) "I've seen the rookie play, and I can't help but admit that he's the best player on the team." (b) "Whenever someone sits beside me on a bus, I can't help but believe that he is from France. Even though I understand that I'm not apprehending anything that makes this likely to be true, someone's sitting next to me on a bus just causes me to believe that he's French." We might say that (a) is an epistemic or rational "can't help but," whereas (b) is a *merely* causal (or compulsive or crazy) one. In (a), the speaker can't help but take matters to be a certain way because he has seen, or takes himself to have seen, that they are that way. In (b), the speaker can't help but take matters to be a certain way because he has got something wrong with him.

The problem with the belief-constitutivist's saying "When I'm exposed to certain stresses, I can't help but believe that I have a headache" is that this use of "can't help but" is like that of the bus passenger—*merely* causal. The belief-constitutivist doesn't take there to be any fact about his own state of mind, the apprehension of which is forcing him to believe that he is in pain. In the context of his theory, his claim that he can't help but think he is suffering a headache amounts to a confession of psychological compulsiveness. The constitutivist who tries to shift the locus of mental state determination from avowals to beliefs ends up with a position according to which our ordinary self-awareness consists of a set of irrational beliefs—beliefs that, were we epistemically responsible, we would rid ourselves of.

We saw earlier that avowal-constitutivism about sensations makes us out to be responsible for our headaches in something like the way in which we are responsible for our actions. What we have just seen is that when a constitutivist moves the locus of determination inside—when he says that it is not our avowals, but our beliefs that determine what we are feeling—he winds up making us out to be responsible for our headaches in a different, but equally unsatisfying, way.

So far we have rejected two versions of constitutivism, both of which aim to explain first-person authority across the whole range of mental states about which we seem to speak with authority. Neither of these positions has much *prima facie* appeal. It seems far more intuitively plausible to say that we constitute our own wishes and intentions than that we constitute our own pains. Thus, if one is drawn to avowal-constitutivism, one will probably be inclined to think that our avowals determine the facts about our own attitudes, but not about our own sensations. A philosopher of this stripe might claim that her position is immune to the objection I raised earlier against avowal-constitutivism about sensations. She might say: "The problem with avowal-constitutivism about sensations is that we are responsible for our avowals, but not for our pains. This is not a problem for me; we *are* responsible for our intentions. (After all, we blame people for having bad intentions.)"[15]

While it is true that we are sometimes held accountable for our intentions, this sort of constitutivism misrepresents our accountability. We rarely blame a person for *avowing* a bad intention. We more typically praise the avowal for its honesty and think ill of the intention itself. But the avowal-constitutivist about intentions cannot draw a line between blaming someone for having a bad intention and blaming him for avowing it. The problem with avowal-constitutivism is that we simply are not responsible for our mental states—sensations, fears, *or* intentions—in the same ways we are responsible for our avowals of them.

---

15. It seems to me that it would be far less tempting, *prima facie*, to say this sort of thing about fear, love, or desire, rather than intention. We often speak with first-person authority about these attitudes even when we are not understood to be responsible or accountable for them in anything like the way we're responsible for our intentions.

It remains for us only to consider belief-constitutivism that is limited to attitudes. According to such a position, when I come to believe that I, e.g., intend to go sailing, my belief constitutively determines that I have this intention. Such a view is susceptible to a version of the objection I raised earlier against belief-constitutivism about sensations. Imagine the following conversation:

> *Belief-constitutivist:* I intend to go sailing this weekend.
> *You:* What brought this on? I thought you hated the water.
> *B-c:* Well, I started to believe that I intend to sail, and such a belief makes itself true.
> *You:* But what led you to believe that about yourself?

The belief-constitutivist might reply that he was causally compelled to believe that he had an intention to sail. But such a belief would be epistemically irresponsible. (The argument here is the same as the one adduced earlier against the belief-constitutivist about sensations.)

*   *   *

In §2.1, we saw that Wright's defense of constitutivism grows out of his reading of Wittgenstein on rule-following; it is motivated as much by a desire to steer clear of platonism as by a concern to explain first-person authority. In §2.2, I argued that we should reject not only Wright's constitutivism, but also the account of meaning and rule-following that lies behind it.

I have just argued that, rules and meaning aside, no form of constitutivism is likely to offer us a satisfactory picture of first-person authority. The moral of the present section could be put this way: constitutivism always misrepresents the kinds of responsibility that we bear for our own states of mind, either by portraying us as active in the constitution of these states when we are not, or by mischaracterizing the ways in which our activity figures in their constitution.

If we reject both detectivism and constitutivism, what are we to think about the relations that a subject bears to his own states of mind? Is there another, better approach toward making sense of them? In the next chapter, I'll discuss a way of understanding the relations we bear to some of our inner states that combines the virtues of detectivism with those of constitutivism while remaining invulnerable to the objections that I've raised against each.

CHAPTER 3

Between Detectivism and Constitutivism

According to detectivism, I am able to speak about my own mental states thanks to a process by which I detect or find out about them. If I speak with a special authority about these states, it is because I have better epistemic access to them than others have; I enjoy something akin to the best *view* of my own interior. In Chapter 1, I distinguished between old and new detectivism. According to old detectivism, my knowledge of my own mental states is of a quite different sort from my knowledge of items that I perceive with my eyes and ears. "Inner sense" provides me with a kind of awareness that is more direct and certain than any visual or auditory awareness. Thus, the connection between my current desire for chocolate and my inner awareness of this desire could be considered more intimate than that between the coffee mug on my desk and my perceptual awareness of it. In what follows, I'll say that a philosopher "acknowledges intimacy" if she holds a view of this sort—one according to which the connection between our states of mind and what we think or say about them is, in some significant way, tighter than the connection between what's on my desk and what I think or say about it. It is, I think, an attractive feature of old detectivism that it comes with an acknowledgment of intimacy. What's unsatisfying about old detectivism is the form that this acknowledgment takes: the old detectivist acknowledges intimacy by positing a supernaturally reliable detection mechanism.

New detectivism renounces old detectivism's appeals to the supernatural. According to new detectivism, we know our own states of mind via the same sorts of natural, fallible cognitive processes that enable us to learn what's going on in the world around us. *Prima facie,* this sounds like a good idea. But in naturalizing detectivism, the new detectivist gives up the old detectivist's acknowledgment of intimacy, and, as we saw in §1.3, this leaves him unable to provide a satisfactory account of first-person authority. We could say that old detectivism is strong on intimacy (insofar as intimacy is, at least, acknowledged by the old detectivist) but weak on naturalness, while new detectivism is strong on naturalness but weak on intimacy.

In these terms, the appeal of constitutivism might be put as follows: we can account for first-person authority in such a way as to respect intimacy *and* naturalness by introducing a constitutive moment into our story about the subject's relations to his own inner states. According to one kind of constitutivism, when I avow that I have, e.g., a particular intention, I make it the case, or help to make it the case, that I do. Such a view acknowledges that the connection between a person's state of mind and what he says about it is, in an important way, tighter than that between the state of his desk and what he says about it, and this acknowledgment comes without the positing of a mind-bogglingly accurate detection mechanism.

In Chapter 2, I argued that any sort of constitutivism has the effect of misrepresenting the subject's responsibility for mental states about which he speaks with first-person authority. The point is perhaps most obvious in connection with an avowal-constitutivism about sensations. If my remarking that I had a headache made it the case that I did have a headache, then sympathy would not be appropriate in response to such a remark. It would, instead, be reasonable to respond along the following lines: "Your headache is your own fault. If you don't want your head to hurt, you shouldn't go around saying that it does." Contrast detectivism: According to detectivism—old or new—I'm able to speak about my inner states thanks to a process by which I cognitively take in (rather than somehow produce) facts about them. Speaking about my headache doesn't require that I be active in its constitution. Thus, no responsibility objection threatens detectivism.

So: old detectivism is strong on intimacy and responsibility but weak on naturalness; new detectivism is strong on naturalness and responsibility but weak on intimacy; and constitutivism is strong on intimacy and naturalness but weak on responsibility. We'd like an approach toward understanding first-person authority that is strong on intimacy, naturalness, *and* responsibility. What might such an approach look like?

Here is a suggestion: Hold on to what's appealing about constitutivism—the idea that we can respect both intimacy and naturalness by introducing a constitutive moment into our story about the relations a subject bears to his own inner states—*without* committing ourselves to the problematic claim that in order for someone to speak with authority about his own state of mind, he must be active in its constitution. (It's this claim that invites one or another form of the responsibility objection.) Is there a way to say both (1) that my awareness of, e.g., my current headache in some sense constitutes it *and* (2) that the constitution of my headache is not due to my activity, so not something for which I am responsible? This chapter will focus on an account of inner awareness according to which both these claims may be true. The account is due to John McDowell, who defends it in his book *Mind and World* as well as in a paper called "One Strand in the Private Language Argument." (McDowell takes Wittgenstein to recommend what amounts to this account of inner awareness in *Philosophical Investigations*. I'll discuss this reading of the *Investigations* in Chapter 6; in the present chapter, I'll be bracketing McDowell's relation to Wittgenstein.)

McDowell's remarks about inner awareness are both penetrating and difficult. I believe that we'll do best to consider them in the context of his related views concerning outer, i.e., perceptual, awareness. In the next two sections, I'll first summarize some of what McDowell says about perceptual awareness and then turn to his views on inner awareness.

3.1. Experience and the Logical Space of Reasons

Let's begin with a fairly uncontroversial point: sensory experience constrains our thinking and judging. I glance out the window of my office and see rain pouring down on the street below. Although I might choose to *imagine* that the sun is shining, my visual experience prevents me from judging or believing that it is. What I judge or believe is constrained by experience in a way that what I merely imagine is not. This sort of constraint is necessary if an exercise of concepts is to constitute a warranted judgment. It would not be possible to gain knowledge of the world via perception if judgment were just as free as imagination—if it were not held in check by the impacts that the world makes on us in experience. McDowell is inclined to put this point in Kantian terms: in order for us to gain perceptual knowledge, the freedom of *spontaneity,* the freedom that attends exercises of our conceptual capacities, must be limited by the deliverances of *receptivity.*[1]

What *kind* of constraint does sensory experience impose on spontaneity? It is here that McDowell thinks many theorists of perception go wrong in either of two ways: by subscribing to the Myth of the Given[2] or by recoiling from the Myth into coherentism. The Myth of the Given—or, anyway, the version of the Myth that McDowell is chiefly concerned to warn against—comprises the following pair of claims taken together:

> *ME* (for "minimal empiricism"):[3] Sensory experience exerts a rational constraint on spontaneity. It provides us with epistemic grounds for judging and thinking what we do.
>
> *NC* (for "nonconceptualism"): Sensory experience is nonconceptual; it does not, in itself, draw conceptual capacities into operation.

The two claims might be elaborated as follows:

> *ME:* We cannot make sense of perceptual knowledge unless we allow that sensory experience imposes rational, as opposed to *merely* causal, con-

---

1. It is helpful to think about "spontaneity" and "receptivity" in terms of the distinction between what is under a subject's control and what is not. What we *receive* in sensory experience is not, in the relevant sense, under our control—not up to us. (This isn't to say that a person cannot, e.g., close her eyes and thereby alter her visual experience. But when she opens them again, she won't get to decide how things appear to her.) If sensory experience *were* up to us, then it could not constrain judgment in such a way as to allow for perceptual knowledge of an objective world. On the other hand, exercises of spontaneity—judgments, for example—are, McDowell says, under our control: "How one's experience represents things to be is not under one's control, but it is up to one whether one accepts the appearance or rejects it" (1996, 11). So, while a person may justly be criticized for judging, e.g., that the two lines in the Müller-Lyre illusion are of different lengths on the basis of appearances that she should have known were misleading, she cannot be so criticized for merely experiencing the illusion (see 1996, 11).

2. The phrase comes from Sellars 1997, a piece that has exerted a pervasive influence on McDowell's thinking.

3. For the phrase "minimal empiricism," see the Introduction to the paperback edition of *Mind and World.*

straints on spontaneity. It must be possible for empirical beliefs to be justified or warranted by the impressions that the world makes on us in, e.g., visual experience. Consider again the situation in which I look out a window and, as a result, come to believe that it is raining. Here, my belief that it is raining is justified by the visual experience that gives rise to it. The fact that it is raining impresses itself upon me, and it is thanks to this visual impression that my belief is justified. Sensory experience gives me *reason* to believe one thing rather than another.

NC: Sensory experience does not, in itself, involve the operation of conceptual capacities. After all, newborn infants—even newborn hamsters—have perceptual experience, yet they are not capable of conceptual thought. Of course, adult humans do bring concepts to bear on the deliverances of the senses, but then, that's just the point: the deliverances of the senses don't, in themselves, involve concepts; concepts must be *brought* to them. Sensory experience is, in itself, brute and inarticulate. Our conceptual capacities are not at work in it.

However appealing each of these claims is, according to McDowell, they cannot both be true for there is no making sense of the idea that experience, conceived of as independent of conceptual occurrences, justifies beliefs or judgments: "[W]e cannot really understand the relations in virtue of which a judgement is warranted except as relations within the space of concepts: relations such as implication or probabilification, which hold between potential exercises of conceptual capacities" (McDowell 1996, 7). I am justified in thinking that it's raining outside because when I look out my window, I have a visual experience *to the effect that* it is raining. Metaphorically speaking, what I think about the weather is warranted by what my perceptual experience *tells* me. But now, if my perceptual experience were nonconceptual, then it could tell me nothing; it would be mute. If experience is to provide me with a reason to believe that such-and-such, it cannot be mute; it must tell me about the layout of reality,[4] so it must draw my conceptual ca-

4. The metaphor of my sensory experience telling me about the layout of reality is potentially misleading. It might suggest a picture in which perceptual knowledge turns out to be more like knowledge by *testimony* than common sense would have it, and this is not McDowell's picture. For McDowell, sensory experience is not an intermediary between subject and world. It is, itself, world-involving; it consists in impressions that the world makes on a subject. To say that my sensory experience tells me that such-and-such is, for McDowell, tantamount to saying that the world tells me that such-and-such *by way of* the impressions it makes on my senses. McDowell's point,

pacities into operation. Brute impacts from the world upon the senses cannot intelligibly be understood to ground my beliefs and judgments. Taken together, ME and NC form a package that is, however tempting, incoherent.

If I were merely caused to say that it was raining by brute impacts from the world upon my body—impacts that, in themselves, didn't involve the actualization of my conceptual capacities—then perhaps I could not be blamed for so "judging," as I would have had no freedom in the matter. Still, while I might be exempt from blame—exculpated—my "opinion" would not be justified. We want a story about perceptual awareness according to which our beliefs may be justified by experience of a reality outside thought. This desire leads us to the idea of the Given, i.e., the package comprising ME and NC. But this idea cannot give us what we want: "In effect, the idea of the Given offers exculpations where we wanted justifications" (McDowell 1996, 8).

*   *   *

If we reject the idea of the Given, how are we to understand perceptual awareness? One option, embraced by Donald Davidson and Richard Rorty, is to reject ME—reject, that is, the thought that perceptual experience ever gives us reason to believe one thing rather than another. According to Davidson (1986), "nothing can count as a reason for holding a belief except another belief" (310; quoted on p. 14 of McDowell 1996).[5] He defends a kind of coherentism, a position according to which the logical space of items that can count as epistemic or theoretical reasons encompasses a rationally coherent network of beliefs and no more. The impressions that the world makes on our senses in experience lie outside this space; they figure in the causal genesis of our beliefs, but they do not constitute reasons for them.

According to Davidson, the idea that our beliefs may be justified by sensory experience (as ME would have it) is a misguided response

---

then, is that the world would be unable to tell me anything by way of the impressions it makes on my senses if these impressions did not involve the operations of my conceptual capacities.

5. McDowell accepts a principle somewhat like this one; we could say that for him, nothing can count as a reason for holding a belief except something that, so to speak, contains a claim. (See McDowell 1998a, 438.) Beliefs contain claims, but, as we'll see, so do sensory impressions as McDowell understands them.

to an epistemic anxiety—an anxiety concerning whether our beliefs about the world constitute genuine knowledge. He aims to show that we can account for the epistemic credentials of our beliefs without thinking of them as rationally related to sensory experience. The details concerning how it is that Davidson thinks this can be accomplished, as well as McDowell's reasons for thinking that Davidson is wrong about this, lie outside the scope of the story I want to tell here. It will suffice to note the following: McDowell believes that Davidson misidentifies what lies behind the appeal of ME and so what really stands in the way of coherentism. According to McDowell, what lies behind the appeal of ME is *not* an anxiety about whether our beliefs constitute genuine knowledge of the world. It is, rather, a concern with how it is possible for us to so much as have beliefs or make judgments at all—how what we we'd like to understand as exercises of concepts can be more than what McDowell likes to call "frictionless spinning in a void." McDowell thinks that Davidson fails to realize that we cannot give up ME without losing our grip on the very intelligibility of contentful belief and judgment. I shall not discuss this difficult point here. For the moment, let's grant it to McDowell and see where he goes with it.

*   *   *

If we cannot deny ME, and the package comprising ME and NC is unacceptable, then we must do without NC. We must, in other words, reject the view that perceptual experience does not, in itself, engage our conceptual capacities. According to McDowell, "[C]onceptual capacities, capacities that belong to spontaneity, are already at work in experiences themselves, not just in judgements based on them" (1996, 24). Thus the way to avoid the Myth of the Given, on the one hand, and coherentism, on the other, is to embrace the idea that perceptual experience is conceptual. According to McDowell, the impressions that the world makes on us in experience just are actualizations, passive engagements, of our conceptual capacities.

Early on in this section, I raised the question of how we should characterize the constraint that perceptual experience imposes on what we are free to judge and believe. Davidson and Rorty would say that this constraint is merely causal. McDowell argues, however, that those who have been taken in by the Myth of the Given have been right to think that this constraint must be rational. What they failed to see is that the only way to make sense of the idea that experience imposes a rational constraint on spontaneity is to reject NC. We must understand the impressions that the world makes on us as already involving our conceptual capacities at work.

The point may be put in terms of what McDowell, following Sellars, calls "the logical space of reasons." Sellars writes: "[I]n characterizing an episode or a state as that of *knowing*, we are not giving an empirical description of that episode or state; we are placing it in the logical space of reasons, of justifying and being able to justify what one says."[6] Although this passage concerns what is involved in characterizing some state as one of *knowing*, McDowell (like Sellars himself) thinks that the point holds for other states as well. To characterize a state as a *believing* that such-and-such is also to locate it in the logical space of reasons. A person who believes that *p* may be called upon to give reasons for believing this; moreover, she may be in a position to cite the fact that *p* as a reason for holding some other belief. According to ME, perceptual impressions figure in the logical space of reasons. To say that someone is under the perceptual impression that it is raining is to say that she has a reason for believing or claiming that it is raining. In these terms, to subscribe to the Myth of the Given is to think that the space of reasons extends beyond what we might call the space of *concepts;* it's to think that something nonconceptual, e.g., a brute impression made by the world upon the senses, can constitute a reason or warrant for believing or judging that such-and-such. According to McDowell, if we are to make sense of empirical knowledge—or even of world-directed thought—we must understand our perceptual impressions as figuring in the logical space of reasons. If we are to avoid the Myth of the Given, then, we must see these impressions as drawing conceptual capacities into play.

3.2. The Middle Path

McDowell points out that the temptation toward the Given, while most familiar in connection with our perceptual knowledge of the world around us, arises as well "in connection with what Kant calls 'inner sense'" (1996, 18). He continues:

6. Sellars 1997, 76; quoted on p. 5 of McDowell 1996.

The realm of thought and judgement includes judgements about the thinker's own perceptions, thoughts, sensations, and the like. The conceptual capacities that are operative in such judgements must belong to spontaneity just as much as any other conceptual capacities do, and that can generate the spectre of a frictionless spinning in a void for this region of thought too. Then, in the way that should by now be familiar, ensuring friction, which is required for genuine content, can seem to oblige us to take exercises of concepts in this region to be rationally grounded in something extra-conceptual, bare presences that are the ultimate grounds of judgements.   (1996, 18)

We subscribe to the Myth of the Given if we imagine that our experience of our own inner states and events, conceived of as extra-conceptual, can ground or justify the judgments that we make about them.

So what does justify such judgments?[7] McDowell recommends that we "think about 'inner sense' in parallel with 'outer sense' to the fullest extent that is possible" (1996, 22). In the case of outer sense,[8] the theorist's task is to understand how our perceptual judgments and beliefs can be rationally constrained by experience of the outer world. In the case of inner sense, the corresponding task is to understand how

7. Four years after *Mind and World,* in his Woodbridge Lectures, McDowell writes: "[T]ypically, perceptual belief acquisition is not a matter of judging, of actively exercising control over one's cognitive life, at all. Unless there are grounds for suspicion, such as odd lighting conditions, having it look to one a certain way—ostensibly seeing things to be that way—becomes accepting that things are that way by a sort of default, involving no exercise of the freedom that figures in a Kantian conception of judgement" (McDowell 1998a, 439). McDowell doesn't comment on whether we acquire beliefs about our own pains and thoughts by this sort of judgment-free default, but it would be odd for him to insist that we do not. Hence, it seems likely that his post–*Mind and World* position is one according to which a subject's coming to believe, e.g., that she herself is in pain does not require that she *judge* herself to be in pain. In order to accommodate this sort of position, the question just posed in the main text might be rewritten as follows: "So what does justify our beliefs about our own inner states?"

8. In *Mind and World,* McDowell usually puts scare-quotes around phrases that involve the words "inner" and "outer." I take it these are meant to remind readers that phrases like "inner sense," "outer sense," and "inner experience" should not be understood, as it were, literally; the word "inner" isn't being used to characterize things that are literally inside the skull (or inside some other, perhaps nonphysical, container). I hope it creates no confusion if I leave off the scare-quotes (except, of course, when I'm directly quoting McDowell) as I have done here.

the judgments that we make about our own "perceptions, thoughts, sensations, and the like" (1996, 18) are rationally constrained by experience of the inner world. We come to understand this, according to McDowell, by conceiving of inner experience, like outer experience, as having conceptual content. What justifies my judgment that I am in pain is an impression of inner sense—understood not as a brute impingement awaiting conceptualization, but as already drawing my conceptual capacities into operation:

> To give the impressions of "inner sense" the right role in justifying judgements, we need to conceive them, like the impressions of "outer sense," as themselves already possessing conceptual content; to supply the necessary limit to the freedom of spontaneity, we need to insist that they are indeed impressions, products of receptivity. So the impressions of "inner sense" must be, like the impressions of "outer sense," passive occurrences in which conceptual capacities are drawn into operation.   (1996, 21–22)

My judgment that I am in pain is justified by an impression *to the effect that I am in pain*—just as my judgment that the cup in front of me is blue is justified by a visual impression whose conceptual content is *that the cup is blue*. Thus, according to McDowell, impressions of inner sense, like impressions of outer sense, have conceptual content. They, as it were, contain claims and so can do justificatory work; they figure in the logical space of reasons.

For all that I have said thus far, McDowell sounds like a new detectivist. He sounds like someone who understands our awareness of our own mental states and events to be on all fours with our perceptual awareness of the goings-on around us. McDowell is not a new detectivist. He takes there to be an important difference between outer and inner sense, viz., that "the objects of 'inner sense' are internal accusatives to the awareness that 'inner experiences' constitute; they have no existence independently of that awareness" (1996, 21).[9] When I see that a cup is blue, the cup's being blue is distinct from my impression that it is. But, according to McDowell, there is no corresponding dis-

9. On the expression "internal accusative": think of sentences like "He smiled a sad smile" or "He sneezed a great sneeze." A grammarian would call the second noun in each sentence an internal accusative.

tinction between an awareness comprising impressions of inner sense and that which the awareness is of. We cannot understand such an awareness to be of "circumstances that obtain in any case and that impress themselves on a subject as they do because of some suitable relation to her sensibility" (1996, 22). He goes on:

> No doubt there are circumstances that obtain in any case, and figure in the aetiology of impressions of "inner sense": for instance, bodily damage in the case of feelings of pain. But if we are to respect the point about internal accusatives, we cannot suppose that such circumstances are objects of an awareness that is constituted by the impressions of "inner sense." . . . If we can make out that judgements of "inner sense" are about anything, it has to be that they are about impressions of "inner sense" themselves, not about something independent of which the impressions constitute awareness. (1996, 22)

Judgments of outer sense are justified by perceptual impressions, but they are not *about* these impressions; they are about the facts that the perceptual impressions are impressions *of*. With respect to inner sense, however, we cannot distinguish between the impressions and that which they are impressions of: "An object of 'inner experience' . . . has no existence independently of the awareness that the experience constitutes" (1996, 36). McDowell sometimes puts the point by saying that inner awareness of, say, pain may be understood as "a limiting case of the structure of awareness and object" (1996, 37–38)—a *limiting* case because "the object of this awareness is really nothing over and above the awareness itself" (1996, 120). The pain in my head is really nothing over and above my conceptual awareness of it. Thus, McDowell's position is not a version of new detectivism because there is a constitutive moment in his account of inner awareness. According to the account, impressions of inner sense, unlike those of outer sense, constitute their objects.

Is McDowell a constitutivist then? Well, it *is* helpful to consider his position alongside those canvassed in Chapter 2. Recall that an avowal-constitutivist holds that what I avow concerning some of my own inner states makes them what they are, while a belief-constitutivist locates the constitutive work, as it were, closer in; she claims that it is what I believe or judge about my inner states that determines what they are. We can think of McDowell as locating the constitutive work in yet another place: what constitutes my thoughts, sensations, etc. is not what I avow *or* believe about them but rather that which, on his view, epistemically justifies what I avow and believe about them, namely, impressions of inner sense.

But while McDowell's position looks, in certain respects, like a kind of constitutivism, it looks like a kind of detectivism as well. A detectivist would claim that I am able to speak about my own inner states by finding out about them. According to McDowell, whether I'm speaking about a possum that I see in my yard or a pain that I feel in my head, I come to know the facts on which I am reporting by receiving sensory impressions—understood as passive occurrences in which conceptual capacities are drawn into play—and by making judgments on their basis.[10] Thus, McDowell offers us a middle path between detectivism and constitutivism. In what follows, I'll refer to this as "the middle path account of inner awareness" or "MPA."

The middle path account of inner awareness seems to combine the appealing features of old detectivism, new detectivism, and constitutivism without suffering from any of their defects. In the introduction to this chapter, I pointed out that an attractive feature of constitutivism is that it allows us to "acknowledge intimacy"—acknowledge, that is, that the connection between my mental states and what I think or say about them is, in some significant way, tighter than the connection between what is on my desk and what I think or say about it—without appealing to any supernaturally reliable inner detection mechanism. But constitutivism misrepresents the kinds of responsibility we bear for our own mental states by misrepresenting our role in their constitution. We are not, as a rule, active in the constitution of our own headaches (and while we *are* active in the constitution of our own intentions, this activity—and so the responsibility that goes with it—is misrepresented by constitutivism). The middle path account of inner awareness allows us to affirm that a subject's awareness of her headache constitutes it, while denying that the headache is due to her activity. What constitutes a pain, according to MPA, is sensory experience, and sensory experience is passive. Thus, I do not turn out to be responsible for my headaches (not *typically;* the account doesn't rule out my turning out to be responsible for a headache that is, e.g., the result of my eating foods

10. Though see n. 7, above.

that tend to give me headaches). Although my awareness constitutes my pain, I am not responsible for my pain because I am passive in the face of it. Thus, McDowell manages to provide an account of inner awareness that is, in the terms of the introduction to this chapter, strong on intimacy, naturalness, *and* responsibility.

MPA exhibits one other significant virtue. McDowell claims (as others have claimed)[11] that pains, tickles, etc. are not independent of our awareness of them. Typically those who say this sort of thing trade on the Myth of the Given; although the having of, e.g., a pain is thought to be independent of the operations of conceptual capacities, somehow it amounts to an awareness—a recognition that a particular is of a certain kind. McDowell sees that this sort of position is hopeless. He finds a way to claim that sensations, etc. are not independent of our awareness of them while steering clear of the Myth. This is no small achievement.

*   *   *

The middle path account of inner awareness allows us to say that we speak with special authority about our own pains because they are constituted by our awareness of them. When someone is in pain, her being in pain is not independent of its seeming to her that she is. Now, would it make sense to say this sort of thing concerning the whole range of mental states about which we speak with first-person authority?

No. Consider intentions. An extension of MPA to intentions would be vulnerable to what we can think of as an inversion of the responsibility objection: such an extension would represent subjects as too free of responsibility for the constitution of their intentions. It is essential to McDowell's story that we are passive in the face of objects of inner sense and so not responsible for them. But that's not how it is with our intentions. We actively formulate them and are held accountable for them, both in courts of law and in our day-to-day dealings with each other. Intentions belong to spontaneity, so there can be no middle path account of our awareness of them.

McDowell's story about inner awareness provides, at best, for a par-

---

11. E.g., Peter Strawson. When McDowell introduces the idea that objects of inner awareness "have no existence independently of that awareness" (1996, 21; see also McDowell 1998d, 284), he cites Strawson 1966, 100–101.

tial understanding of first-person authority. It extends, he says, to "perceptions, thoughts, sensations, and the like" (1996, 18)[12]—mental phenomena that are, as it were, *all there* in (what might be thought of as) the stream of consciousness. Even if we accept that McDowell provides us with all that we need in order to understand the authority with which one speaks about such items, we shall still have to face the question of how to account for the authority with which one speaks about one's own intentions and beliefs. Still, a partial solution to our problem would seem to be a good deal better than no solution at all.

3.3. When a Dog Feels Pain

One difficulty with the middle path account of inner awareness is that it seems to leave little room for the sentience of brutes. McDowell characterizes experience, both inner and outer, as constituted by the actualization of conceptual capacities. Animals without conceptual capacities do not so much as *have* experience on this conception of it.[13] This, McDowell notes, "can seem to commit me to the Cartesian idea that brutes are automata" (1996, 114).

The difficulty is particularly acute in connection with the experience of inner items. Although McDowell would deny that brutes enjoy full-fledged visual *experience,* he notes that they are visually *sensitive* to features of their environments. Thus, my dog and I can be said to *see* the same tree. But, according to MPA, when I feel a pain, I have experience of something in me that is entirely constituted by the actualization of my conceptual capacities. A creature without conceptual capacities (my dog, say) could neither experience nor be sensitive to such a thing's presence in her—because there could *be* no such thing present in her. Thus, while there is room for McDowell to say that dogs see trees, there is, apparently, no room for him to say that they feel pains.

I take it that McDowell's reply to this line of thought would be that its conclusion is a *non sequitur.* His view is that *some* pains, ours, are constituted by the actualization of conceptual capacities. Other pains, those of brutes, are not. There is, then, an important difference be-

12. Later in the book, the list reads, "Sensations, emotional states, and the like" (1996, 119).

13. Moreover, according to McDowell, any animal without language has no conceptual capacities.

tween the kind of pain I feel and the kind felt by my dog. But it doesn't follow that my dog cannot feel pain:

> Only for a full-fledged subjectivity can what it is to feel pain or fear amount to a limiting-case awareness of a degeneratively substantial inner state of affairs. The limiting case of the structure of awareness and object is in place only because of how the awareness is structured by understanding. But nothing in the concepts of pain or fear implies that they can get a grip only where there is understanding, and thus full-fledged subjectivity. There is no reason to suppose that they can be applied in a non-first-person way only to something capable of applying them to itself in a first-person way.   (1996, 120–121)

When one acquires the concept *pain*, one learns how to apply it both to oneself and to others. Applying it to others is, in part, a matter of recognizing expressions of pain in one's fellow creatures. According to McDowell, if I hear a wounded person cry out, I might apply the concept *pain* to someone whose pain just is a certain sort of conceptual episode. When I hear a wounded dog cry out, I may rightly apply the same concept, even though the dog's pain cannot be understood in just the same way.

It is difficult to formulate a decisive objection to this way of reconciling the middle path account of inner awareness with the fact that dogs feel pain. Rather than pursue such an objection at this point, I am going to leave off the discussion of animals for a while and raise a different sort of worry about MPA. I'll say more about McDowell on the sentience of brutes in Chapter 6.

3.4. The Phantom Smell Objection

As we have seen, McDowell claims that a person's pain or fear is nothing over and above her awareness of it. It might seem, then, that were we able to imagine a case in which someone was unaware of her own pain or fear, this would pose a serious problem for him. With respect to fear, few philosophers (and even fewer psychoanalysts) would deny that such cases are easy to come by; we are often unaware of our own fears. Moreover, some philosophers would claim that we may be unaware of our own pains as well. David Armstrong is a case in point. He writes:

> Suppose . . . the following dissociated state occurred. A person goes through many of the physical routines associated with pain. At the same time, however, the person denies having a pain, and the denial appears to be sincere. One could imagine such a person passing the most sophisticated tests for the detection of lies. One can imagine also that when the person is faced with the paradox of the combination of the denials and the pain-behaviour, he reacts with incomprehension. Perhaps he is not even aware of the pain-behaviour.
>
> In these circumstances, at least one reasonable way of explaining what was going on would be that the person had a severe pain but was unaware of having it.   (Armstrong and Malcolm 1984, 133)

Does McDowell's middle path account of inner awareness commit him to denying that the person described by Armstrong might reasonably be said to be in pain? Does it commit him even to denying that there exist unconscious fears?

No. McDowell needn't deny that a person may be unaware of her own fear or pain. He simply needs to distinguish between *this* sort of pain or fear and the sort with which he is concerned. What's moving McDowell is a worry about how to understand a kind of *awareness*— awareness of items that might be understood as figuring in a stream of consciousness. He thinks that where a subject has such an awareness, we must understand the object of awareness as already involving concepts, else we succumb to the Myth of the Given. But if there are cases in which someone can rightly be said to have a pain of which she is unaware, this raises no real difficulty for McDowell. If, for example, someone reports on the basis of another's testimony that she writhed in pain all night in her sleep, McDowell need not deny her claim or insist that she *was* aware of the pain even though she was sleeping. In such a case, there is no temptation to say that someone *knows* or is *justified* in believing something about herself on the basis of a nonconceptual occurrence in consciousness. The Myth of the Given is not at issue. McDowell holds that brutes feel pains of which they are not aware— pains of a different sort from the pain I feel if I stub my toe or get a headache. He can say the same thing if he is presented with a case in which a *person* may be said to have pains (or fears) of which she is unaware.

If we seek a convincing objection to the middle path account of inner awareness, we'll need another sort of example, one that involves a sensation of which the subject is *not* unaware. So: imagine a person—call him Cyrano—who occasionally experiences what might be called a "phantom smell"; it seems to him that there is an odd, somewhat unpleasant odor in the air when there is really no such odor present. (In fact, this sort of thing does occur and may be a symptom of a brain tumor.) When Cyrano tries to describe the character of this peculiar olfactory sensation, perhaps to a neurologist, he feels frustrated; it seems to him that he is unable to capture it in words. He says, "Well, the smell is a bit unpleasant, though not terrible. Still, it's pretty strong. I just don't know how to tell you what it's like." One morning, Cyrano experiences the phantom smell and tells his cousin Roxanne about it. That afternoon, the two of them take a walk in the park. There, Cyrano encounters the first wet dogs he's ever had a sniff at. (Or perhaps he encountered wet dogs as an infant, but not since then.) He remarks excitedly: "That strange olfactory sensation I told you about this morning—it was the smell of wet dog." (Perhaps developmental psychologists will discover that people who are exposed to certain smells as infants often have phantom versions of them later in life. Perhaps, given Cyrano's background and heredity, it was even predictable that as an adult, he would experience phantom doggy-smells.) So: at (let us say) 10 A.M., Cyrano has a sensation of a particular kind; call it "doggy-smelling" (or just "doggy"). Later in the day, at 3 P.M., he first becomes aware that the sensation he had at 10 was doggy.

We can begin to appreciate how this story poses a real problem for the middle path account of inner awareness by comparing it with one that does not. Imagine that one afternoon I say to a friend, "I had a throbbing pain in my wrist this morning." Imagine, moreover, that in so saying, I am speaking honestly about a sensation that I did in fact experience and now remember. If MPA is correct, the sensation I had in the morning was partly constituted by the actualization in me of the concept *throbbing*. In the afternoon, when I tell my friend about it, my remark is epistemically justified in part by virtue of my remembering the actualization of this concept. In the morning, the sensation impressed itself upon me *as* throbbing, and later, I remember this impression. Notice that the phantom smell story cannot be understood in the same way. When Cyrano says, in effect, that the sensation he experienced earlier in the day was doggy-smelling, he is not remembering a sensation that was partly constituted by the actualization of the concept *doggy-smelling*. At 10 A.M., he didn't *have* the concept *doggy-*

smelling; he didn't know that wet dogs have a distinctive smell. What, then, justifies the assertion that Cyrano makes in the afternoon about the sensation he experienced in the morning? And how can it be that this sensation—which, after all, was an occurrent item in consciousness (unlike, say, an unconscious fear)—was nothing over and above his conceptualizing of it?

*   *   *

I don't believe that a proponent of MPA can offer a satisfactory answer to either of the questions just posed. To see that this is so, let us consider a couple of approaches that one might take in trying to answer them. The first, which could be called "the retroactive approach," might be stated as follows: "According to MPA, our sensations are actualizations of our conceptual capacities and nothing more. We can hold onto this thought in the face of the phantom smell example if we understand Cyrano's olfactory sensation to be partly constituted by—indeed, doggy by virtue of—the conceptualizing of it *as* doggy that comes several hours *after* its occurrence. In the afternoon, it becomes the case that, in the morning, Cyrano's sensation *was* doggy. And when he says to his cousin, 'That weird olfactory sensation . . . was the smell of wet dog,' his assertion is justified by virtue of a conceptual impression that partly constitutes its object *retroactively*."

It seems to me that the more one reflects on this approach toward meeting the challenge raised by the phantom smell example, the less intelligible it appears to be. When, at 3 P.M., Cyrano announces that the olfactory sensation he had in the morning was just like the smell of wet dog, he means to be describing the character of an episode that is over and done with. If Roxanne were to reply that the sensation in question was doggy only thanks to his current exposure to dogs, Cyrano might well complain that she has no good reason to distrust his *memory*. And if, at this point, she were to say (perhaps in a reassuring tone of voice), "I trust your memory, and I accept that your olfactory sensation this morning *was* doggy; I'm merely suggesting that what *made* it doggy was what happened just now," I imagine that Cyrano would respond with an expression of incomprehension. He might say: "You're granting that my sensation, which lasted only a minute or two this morning, really and truly had a certain distinct qualitative character—it was doggy—*while* claiming that if I hadn't come to the park this afternoon, that very sensation would not have been at all doggy. I simply can't get my mind around that. I feel as though you're trying, but not at all hard, to *humor* me—as though you're pretending to grant me a claim, while denying it in the same breath."

It *does* make a kind of sense to say, "That woman's dying makes it the case that what her husband did six hours ago was murder." But the grammar of sensations just isn't like this. We don't know how to make sense of the suggestion that a sensation *awaits completion* in the way that a murder does.

By the way, I don't believe that McDowell would be at all attracted to the retroactive approach toward defending his position. Consider what he has to say about Crispin Wright's claim (discussed in Chapter 2) that our intentions may be retroactively constituted by judgments that we make about them after the fact:

> [S]urely nobody but a philosopher would entertain the thesis that we have to wait and see whether what we find ourselves to have done strikes us as an execution of our intention before it can be determinate what our intention is. (McDowell 1998e, 53)

McDowell would, I imagine, say the same thing about sensations (for which the idea of retroactive constitution is, it seems to me, even less appealing): nobody but a philosopher would entertain the thesis that we have to wait and see whether a sensation later strikes us as *doggy-smelling* before it can be determinate whether it is.

*   *   *

How else might a defender of MPA try to come to grips with the phantom smell example? The second approach I'd like you to consider parallels a line of thought that McDowell sets out in opposition to Gareth Evans. Evans argues that perceptual experiences are nonconceptual by pointing out that most people can discriminate many more shades of color than they have words for. He takes this to show that our repertoire of color concepts is coarser in grain than our experience of colors. McDowell disagrees. He argues that it's a mistake to think we have only as many color concepts as we have color *words*—for one may acquire a color concept by exploiting the presence of a sample whose shade one refers to demonstratively:

> But why should we accept that a person's ability to embrace colour within her conceptual thinking is restricted to concepts expressible by

words like "red" or "green" and phrases like "burnt sienna"? It is possible to acquire the concept of a shade of colour, and most of us have done so. Why not say that one is thereby equipped to embrace shades of colour within one's conceptual thinking with the very same determinateness with which they are presented in one's visual experience, so that one's concepts can capture colours no less sharply than one's experience presents them? In the throes of an experience of the kind that putatively transcends one's conceptual powers—an experience that *ex hypothesi* affords a suitable sample—one can give linguistic expression to a concept that is exactly as fine-grained as the experience, by uttering a phrase like "that shade," in which the demonstrative exploits the presence of the sample.   (1996, 56–57)

A defender of MPA might employ a related strategy when confronted with the phantom smell example. He might say: "Cyrano's olfactory sensation at 10 A.M. was nothing over and above the conceptual awareness he had of it *then,* at 10 A.M. But although at 10 A.M. Cyrano would have had trouble communicating the precise character of his sensation to a neurologist, he already had a fine-grained demonstrative concept that figured in his awareness of it. He could have given linguistic expression to this concept with the help of a phrase like 'that odor': at 10 A.M., he might have said, 'There's that odor again.' At 3 P.M., Cyrano recognizes the wet dogs in the park as falling under this already acquired concept; he thereby learns that wet dogs have *that* odor, and this is what justifies his remark to his cousin." Call this "the demonstrative approach" to the phantom smell example.

While this way of defending MPA might seem to parallel closely McDowell's way of answering Evans, there are important differences. In the sort of case at issue in the long passage from McDowell quoted above, there is in view of a perceiver a colored object that has its shade independently of her awareness of it. This object (say, a blue truck) makes it possible for her to have a determinate thought that takes this form: "I want *that* shade of blue for the walls of my bathroom." The color of the truck, as it were, *gives content to* her demonstrative. Now, what's supposed to correspond to this colored object in the phantom smell case is Cyrano's olfactory sensation. But a proponent of MPA holds that the character of such a sensation (unlike the color of a truck) is not independent of a subject's conceptual awareness of it. And herein lies the problem with this strategy for defending MPA. A philosopher who takes the demonstrative approach to the phantom smell example will want to say that at 10 A.M., Cyrano experiences his phantom olfactory sensation as falling under a fine-grained demonstrative concept that (1) he can give expression to by making use of the phrase "that odor," (2) he only later learns applies to wet dogs, and (3) has its determinate, fine-grained content thanks to the doggy character of the phantom olfactory sensations that he's been experiencing for the past few weeks. But if he does say this, he must *reject* MPA, for he cannot, without falling into a vicious circle, *also* say that the doggy character of these sensations depends upon the content of the demonstrative concept. If the demonstrative derives its content from the determinate olfactory character of the presented sample, the sample's olfactory character cannot depend on the demonstrative's content.

Thus, the demonstrative approach toward reconciling the middle path account of inner awareness with the phantom smell example should be rejected along with the retroactive approach. And I can think of no third approach whose prospects seem any brighter. What is it that justifies Cyrano when he says that his phantom olfactory sensation was doggy? And how can it be that this sensation—which was doggy before he was aware of it as such—could have been nothing over and above his conceptual awareness of it? The middle path account of inner awareness lacks the resources either to answer or to dismiss these questions. The case of Cyrano thus constitutes a counterexample to MPA. It suggests that there is, or may be, more to an occurrent item in consciousness than a subject's conceptual awareness of it.[14]

3.5. Back to Detectivism?

In the face of the phantom smell objection, we might be tempted to embrace what could be thought of as a McDowellian kind of new

14. The phantom smell objection does not speak against McDowell's discussion of outer awareness in *Mind and World*—only against the way in which the morals of this discussion are brought to bear on the topic of *inner* awareness. Moreover, and perhaps contrary to first appearances, it is not a simple matter to recast the objection so that it does speak against what McDowell has to say about outer, perceptual awareness. Indeed, I don't take what I'm doing here (in this book) to constitute a criticism of any of the *main* lines of thought in *Mind and World,* and it would neither surprise nor displease me if my efforts had the effect of making these lines of thought seem *more* attractive to some readers. (I'll say a little bit more about this in §6.4.)

detectivism. Imagine a philosopher who says: "The claims I make about my own sensations are justified in the same way as claims I make about the outer world—thanks to conceptual impressions that are independent of their objects. McDowell is right to insist that we need to understand sensory impressions as conceptual in order to avoid the Myth of the Given. But we should reject the idea that impressions of inner sense constitute their objects." A detectivist who said this could be characterized as *McDowellian* because she would accept (1) what McDowell has to say about the need to understand sensory impressions as conceptual in order to avoid falling into the Myth of the Given and (2) that self-ascriptions of pain, etc. are justified by such impressions. She would diverge from McDowell in rejecting the middle path account of inner awareness; on her view, impressions of inner sense no more constitute their objects than do impressions of outer sense.

While the phantom smell example would present no special difficulty for our McDowellian new detectivist, we have already given a label to what goes missing in her position: she fails to make room for what, in the introduction to this chapter, I called an "acknowledgment of intimacy." On her view, the connection between my pain and what I say or think about it is no tighter—no more intimate—than that between the state of my desk and what I say or think about it.[15] Our reasons for becoming dissatisfied with new detectivism in Chapter 1 did not depend on the new detectivist's subscribing to the Myth of the Given. If we find ourselves sliding back toward new detectivism now, it is only because we seem to have run out of options. Detectivism and constitutivism are both unsatisfactory, as is the middle path between them. Is there a better way to make sense of the relations that we bear to our own inner states? In the three chapters still to come, I'll argue that there is.

15. McDowell himself would reject any account of inner awareness that failed to acknowledge intimacy. He notes that if we were to hold that "a subject registers his mental goings-on in the way that he registers, say, the state of the weather, we would lose the interiority of the states of affairs in question. It would not help to insist that they can still be first-personal if this comes to no more than the sense in which, say, my needing a haircut is first-personal. (It is not 'from inside' that I know that I need a haircut.)" (McDowell 1998b, 312).

Expression

CHAPTER 4

Meaning, Expression, and Expressivism

In Part I, I argued against old and new detectivism, various sorts of constitutivism, and the middle path account of inner awareness. I urged you to reject what Crispin Wright has to say about the authority with which we avow our own wishes, fears, and intentions, as well as what John McDowell has to say about our awareness of our own pains and other occurrent inner items. In Part II, I'll set out what I take to be a better approach toward understanding the relations that we bear to our own inner states.

I agree with Wright about two things: First, insofar as we are concerned to make sense of first-person authority, we can benefit from taking seriously what Wittgenstein thinks about the self-ascription of mental states. Second, if we hope to take seriously what Wittgenstein thinks about the self-ascription of mental states, we should attend to his remarks on rule-following. Wright sees that there is an important connection between these two strands in Wittgenstein's thought, even if, as I shall argue, he misrepresents both of them. In the present chapter, I'll discuss Wittgenstein's related views on (1) rule-following, (2) expression, and (3) the self-ascription of mental states.

4.1. Meaning

I should begin by reviewing briefly some of what was said in Chapter 2 concerning Wittgenstein's remarks on rule-following. In *PI* §431, Wittgenstein's interlocutor articulates what might seem to be an innocuous thought:

> "There is a gulf between an order and its execution. It has to be filled by the act of understanding."

Understood in a certain way, what's said here really *is* innocuous. It does sometimes happen that a person is given an order that he does not understand and so cannot execute. In such a circumstance, it might be said that there is a gulf between the order and its execution—a gulf that may be bridged with the help of an interpretation that the order's recipient is able to grasp (in an "act of understanding"). In §2.2, I offered the example of an American tourist in Rome who manages, perhaps with the help of an English-Italian dictionary, to interpret an order shouted at her by an Italian policeman. This interpretation helps to bridge the gulf between the policeman's order and its execution.

But the interlocutor's point in §431 is not merely that such gulfs *sometimes* open up; it is, rather, that *whenever* an order is issued, there is a gulf of understanding between it and its execution. This is apparent in the continuation of §431:

> "Only in the act of understanding is it meant that we are to do THIS.
> The *order*——why, that is nothing but sounds, ink-marks."

The thought expressed here might be put as follows: "Any order (or instruction or statement of a rule) is, in itself, just a string of sounds or marks, and such a string can be understood in all sorts of ways. No particular meaning can be intrinsic to a series of noises or marks on a page. For an order, *any* order, to call for one thing rather than another, it must be supplemented by an act of understanding. So, really, you are always in a position akin to that of the American tourist in Rome. You cannot follow even a simple English instruction—e.g., 'Please stay seated'—without first attaching the right interpretation to it."

Once we have accepted that there is, in this way, a gulf between every order and its execution, it is hard to see how any such gulf could be bridged. If "Please stay seated" can be misunderstood, so too can any interpretation that is attached to these words. Such an interpretation will stand in as much need of interpretation as that which it purports to be an interpretation of. If every order comes with a gulf, then so too does every interpretation. Thus, each interpretation seems to require another standing behind it, and the gulf between order and execution is never bridged.

In Chapter 2, I said that the "paradox" of *PI* §201—"no course of action could be determined by a rule, because every course of action can be made out to accord with the rule"—has its roots in the thought that there is, in every case, a gulf between the statement of a rule and its application. *Prima facie*, it hardly seems as if every course of action can be made out to accord with every rule. Imagine that the following rule is posted at the entrance to a roller coaster: "Please stay seated while the roller coaster is in motion." Imagine further that, while the roller coaster is in motion, a passenger unbuckles his harness and stands up on his seat. How can *this* behavior be made out to accord with *that* rule? The paradox of §201 gains a foothold once we have accepted a thought that might be put as follows: "The words 'Please stay seated while the roller coaster is in motion' are, in themselves, just bits of dried paint on a piece of wood. Without interpretation, they don't call for one course of action any more than another." I shall argue that Wittgenstein avoids the paradox of *PI* §201 by questioning and ultimately rejecting the impulse to say this sort of thing (the impulse to say, e.g., "The *order*——why, that is nothing but sounds, ink-marks"). But there are other ways of responding to the regress of interpretations and the paradox of *PI* §201.

One is platonism. A platonist tries to block the regress and avoid the paradox by positing regress-*stoppers*—intrinsically significant items that lie hidden behind our words. These items differ from mere utterances, inscriptions, and gestures in that they neither need nor brook interpretation. We saw in Chapter 2 that Wright and Wright's Wittgenstein reject platonism and propose yet another response to the paradox: our best judgments concerning the question of whether some bit of behavior accords with a rule determine, rather than reflect, whether the behavior does indeed accord with the rule. These judgments, which can seem to be tracking independent matters of fact, are, rather, stipulative; they *fix* whether or not a given bit of behavior is in accord with a particular rule. In §2.2, I argued that this sort of response to the paradox either falls prey to a version of the regress of interpretations or itself amounts to a kind of platonism. So much by way of review.

*   *   *

Wright admits that there is some textual evidence to support a rather different way of understanding what Wittgenstein is up to. According to what he calls "'official' Wittgensteinianism" (2001e, 189), we should accept that there are facts about what our words mean (what our rules call for, etc.), while rejecting the demand for a constitutive account of that by virtue of which they mean what they do: "Asked what constitutes the truth of rule-informed judgment of the kind we isolated, the official Wittgensteinian will reply: 'Bad question, leading to bad philosophy—Platonism, for instance, or Kripkean scepticism'" (Wright 2001e, 211). The problem with taking up this stance, according to Wright, is that it requires us to turn our faces away from a question that might, after all, yield a philosophically illuminating answer. To Wright, "official" Wittgensteinianism seems to amount to a kind of avoidance of philosophy. According to "official" readings of him, Wittgenstein refuses to answer constitutive questions about meaning. As Wright sees things, the "official" Wittgenstein thereby fails to rise to "the challenge posed by his own thought" (Wright 2001a, 169). Thus, when Wright is introducing his own non-"official" reading of Wittgenstein, he writes:

> I want to canvass a third possibility: an account of the central insight of Wittgenstein's discussion of rule-following which is neither Kripkean nor 'official.' It may be that the 'official' view is exegetically correct, and that I do here part company with the intentions of the actual, historical Wittgenstein. But it seems to me that it is an important methodological precept that we do not despair of giving answers to constitutive questions too soon; if the accomplishments of analysis in philosophy often seem meagre, that may be because it is difficult, not impossible. (Wright 2001e, 191)

Soon, I shall claim that Wright does indeed "part company with the intentions of the actual, historical Wittgenstein." Although Wright acknowledges this possibility—although he sees that the actual, historical Wittgenstein might have rejected constitutive questions about meaning—he never gets in view the kind of rejection that is at issue in Wittgenstein's texts. To Wright, it appears that if we seek to avoid scepticism and platonism, we have just two options: either we must try to articulate that in which meaning one thing rather than another consists, or we must (with the "official" Wittgenstein) opt for "quietism" (1989, 305) and refuse to engage with what is, after all, a gripping question. In what remains of this section, I'll argue that Wittgenstein would reject both horns of this dilemma.

*   *   *

In response to Kripke's commentary on the *Investigations,* which is generally read as suggesting that the first paragraph of §201 (that in which the paradox is stated) articulates the main conclusion of the book, a number of writers have pointed out that the second paragraph rejects the line of thought expressed in the first:[1]

> It can be seen that there is a misunderstanding here from the mere fact that in the course of our argument we give one interpretation after another; as if each one contented us at least for a moment, until we thought of yet another standing behind it. What this shews is that there is a way of grasping a rule which is *not* an *interpretation,* but which is exhibited in what we call "obeying the rule" and "going against it" in actual cases.

The second paragraph of §201 indicates that, according to Wittgenstein, the paradox stated in the first paragraph reflects a misunderstanding. The paradox depends upon our thinking that the grasping of every rule requires that it first be interpreted. On the reading of Wittgenstein that Wright recommends, one grasps a rule without interpreting it by deciding what it requires. I take it, however, that Wittgenstein would have us avoid the paradox not by finding a noninterpretative way to bridge a gulf between a rule and its application, but by coming to question the idea that every rule comes with such a gulf. We are led to this idea by a pair of related arguments:

(1) Where it is possible to misapply a rule—and this is always possible—understanding requires that the rule be supplemented. An "act of understanding" is needed in order to ensure that there will be no mistakes in the application of the rule. We see, e.g., that the teacher's order in *PI* §185 *might* be interpreted to mean that one should write "1004" after "1000," and we infer that the order can be grasped only by someone who gives it an adequate interpretation, or something like an interpretation—a stipulation, perhaps.

(2) In itself, any rule is just a sequence of meaningless noises or ink-

1. See, e.g., McDowell 1998f and McGinn 1984.

marks (or bodily movements). Something must be added to such items if they are to *call for* one activity rather than another. So (once again), an "act of understanding" is needed in order to bridge the gulf between a rule—viewed as noises or ink-marks—and any determinate set of requirements.

As I read Wittgenstein, both of these arguments are under attack. Let's begin with (1). At *PI* §85, Wittgenstein writes: "A rule stands there like a sign-post.—Does the sign post leave no doubt open about the way I have to go? . . . But where is it said which way I am to follow it; whether in the direction of its finger or (e.g.) in the opposite one?" It is *possible* that on seeing a signpost in the road, someone with no experience of signposts would take it to be pointing in the direction opposite to its finger. But this doesn't mean that for most of us such a signpost needs to be supplemented by an interpretation or an explanation in order for it to be understood. For most of us, a signpost is clear enough:

> Suppose I give this explanation: "I take 'Moses' to mean the man, if there was such a man, who led the Israelites out of Egypt, whatever he was called then and whatever he may or may not have done besides."—But similar doubts to those about "Moses" are possible about the words of this explanation (what are you calling "Egypt," whom the "Israelites" etc.?). Nor would these questions come to an end when we got down to words like "red," "dark," "sweet."—"But then how does an explanation help me to understand, if after all it is not the final one? In that case the explanation is never completed; so I still don't understand what he means, and never shall!"—As though an explanation as it were hung in the air unless supported by another one. Whereas an explanation may indeed rest on another one that has been given, but none stands in need of another—unless *we* require it to prevent a misunderstanding. One might say: an explanation serves to remove or to avert a misunderstanding——one, that is, that would occur but for the explanation; not every one that I can imagine.
>
> It may easily look as if every doubt merely *revealed* an existing gap in the foundations; so that secure understanding is only possible if we first doubt everything that *can* be doubted, and then remove all these doubts.
>
> The sign-post is in order—if, under normal circumstances, it fulfills its purpose. (*PI* §87)

An interpretation is a kind of explanation. It makes sense to provide an interpretation of a sentence (or a signpost) when someone has misunderstood it or when there's a real danger that someone will misunderstand it. This is where interpretation has, as it were, its home. When doing philosophy, however, we find ourselves insisting that interpretation is called for wherever we can *imagine* a misunderstanding. An adequate interpretation, we think, is one that would eliminate all chance of anyone's misapplying a sentence or rule. This reflects a misunderstanding about the purpose of interpretation. Once we have succumbed to this misunderstanding, interpretation stops making sense to us. It looks pointless.

A child might misunderstand the instruction "Beat six egg whites until stiff peaks form." (She might have no idea that eggs can be separated. She might think "stiff" means *stiff as a board*.) It doesn't follow that *I* need an interpretation in order to understand these words when I encounter them in a cookbook. For me, there is no gulf between such an instruction and what it requires; I see what it calls for—without the need for interpretation or explanation.

At this point, someone might introduce a version of argument (2) from above: "But isn't the instruction in your recipe book really just a series of dead ink-marks? Don't you need to interpret the marks in order to bring them to life? Or if it isn't interpretation that brings a sign to life, mustn't it then be an assignment of meaning—a stipulation?"

At *PI* §432, Wittgenstein writes:

> Every sign *by itself* seems dead. *What* gives it life?—In use it is *alive.*

Wittgenstein does not agree that signs are dead until we interpret them or stipulate what they mean. A sign only *seems* dead if we consider it *by itself*—i.e., apart from the use that we make of it. In its use, a sign lives. The following passage has a similar moral:

> How does it come about that this arrow >>>——> *points?* . . . The arrow points only in the application that a living being makes of it.   (*PI* §454)

If we view the arrow as cut off from the activities of human beings, it *will* seem that only an interpretation or a stipulation could give it life—could make it point. As we've seen, we cannot provide a general account of how signs get their meaning by appealing to interpretation or stipulation. The conclusion that Wittgenstein draws from this is not that we must succumb to scepticism about meaning—succumb, that is, to the view that signs are in fact dead. Rather, Wittgenstein would have us realize that we need not view the arrow as cut off from the activities of living beings. "In use it is *alive.*"

Are written words really just dead ink-marks—squiggles on the page? I've noticed that if I stare at written English words for a long time, they begin to *seem* like squiggles. (It helps to squint a little.) But it makes sense for me to say this only thanks to the *distinction* between squiggles and English words. My copy of *The Joy of Cooking* does contain ink-marks, but ink-marks of *that* sort figure in our lives in all sorts of ways that meaningless squiggles don't. If a book contained *mere* ink-marks—empty squiggles—it would be very odd to suggest that someone should try to *follow* some of them.

Wittgenstein is continually reminding us that the phenomena in which he is interested—providing interpretations, ostensively defining, reading, making a move in a game of chess, expecting an explosion, feeling pain—make sense only when "surrounded by certain normal manifestations of life" (Z§534). As long as we try to "undress" words—to strip away the context and understand them as squiggles—we will be unable to make sense of the suggestion that "there is a way of grasping a rule which is *not* an *interpretation.*" How could someone understand a squiggle unless he first attached some interpretation to it? By stipulation? If someone merely *stipulates* that a squiggle means, e.g., *Dice three medium onions,* he isn't *understanding* a recipe; he's making one up. (And if *these* words are just noises, he's not even managing that.) When I open a cookbook and see "Beat six egg whites," I don't encounter a squiggle; in the context of the way we live with words, recipes, food, kitchens, and one another, that sentence calls for a quite specific activity.[2] Strip away the context, however, and you won't be able to make sense of the idea that the ink-marks which remain call for me to do anything.

The thought that, in reality, words are no more than squiggles has come to seem innocuous to many contemporary philosophers. But the thought is *not* innocuous; it causes us to lose our grip on important

2. This is not to deny that there is a *subpersonal* story to be told by cognitive psychology about how my visual system processes patterns of light and dark when I read a book. But when I peruse *The Joy of Cooking, I* don't interpret patterns of light and dark. I see instructions. (My seeing instructions is made possible by—among other things—my visual system's processing patterns of light and dark.)

distinctions—such as that between vague, imperspicuous instructions (e.g., a rule that calls for "orderly" behavior from students) and clear, precise ones, such as are found in most cookbooks. While the former stand in need of supplementation—interpretation or stipulation—the latter generally do not. We might say that a cookbook's instructions autonomously call for quite specific activities in the kitchen.

*   *   *

Wright's Wittgenstein hears any talk of a rule's autonomously calling for one activity rather than another as an expression of platonism:

> Platonism is, precisely, the view that the correctness of a rule-informed judgment is a matter quite independent of any opinion of ours, whether the states of affairs which confer correctness are thought of as man-made—constituted by over-and-done-with episodes of explanation and linguistic behaviour—or truly platonic and constituted in heaven.   (Wright 2001e, 210)

> [W]e have no model of what constitutes the direction taken by a rule . . . once the direction is conceived, after the fashion of platonism, as determined autonomously. . . .   (Wright 2001a, 161)

These passages express a misunderstanding of the role that the platonist plays in Wittgenstein's dialectic. The "platonist," insofar as this term is supposed to name someone who figures as a target in Wittgenstein's dialectic, is not merely someone who allows himself to say that a rule autonomously calls for this or that. Wittgenstein's platonist is someone who, first, agrees that there is a gulf between any rule and its application and, then, imagines items that have a mysterious power to bridge the gulf. (Moreover the platonist imagines that he *explains* something by saying that certain items have this power. He claims to explain the connection between a rule and its application by saying, in effect: "Certain items have the power to reach out to all of their applications." The problem with saying this is *not* that there are no items which can be said, innocently, to reach out to their applications [rules *are* such items!], but that the platonist has done nothing more than describe what he promised to explain—adding, misleadingly, that what's going on is mysterious.)

Let us consider again *PI* §454—the section about the arrow's pointing—this time looking at a bit more of it:

How does it come about that this arrow >>>——> *points?* Doesn't it seem to carry in it something besides itself?—"No, not the dead line on paper; only the psychical thing, the meaning, can do that."—That is both true and false. The arrow points only in the application that a living being makes of it.

This pointing is *not* a hocus-pocus which can be performed only by the soul.

As we saw above, the question about how the arrow manages to point arises because we are inclined to view it as a dead mark on paper; we forget that such marks have a life in the activities of human beings. The platonist is someone who, seeing the arrow as dead, supposes that it manages to point thanks to some "psychical thing" associated with it. This account of how the arrow points looks spooky even to the platonist himself. In viewing our words as dead noises and marks, the platonist imagines them divorced from the practices in which they participate and the states of mind that they express. This leaves both words *and* states of mind seeming unconnected to anything. What Wittgenstein calls "the weave of our life"[3] comes to seem unraveled, and its strands—whether they be items encountered on the page or in the mind—seem incapable of meaning anything. The platonist maintains that even so, words and thoughts somehow manage to have content, but it seems mind-boggling to him that they should.

According to Wittgenstein, the platonist isn't wrong in thinking that our words and thoughts have content; he's wrong to find it mind-boggling that they should. Consider the following from *PI* §195:

> "But I don't mean that what I do now (in grasping a sense) determines the future use *causally* and as a matter of experience, but that in a *queer* way, the use itself is in some sense present."—But of course it is, 'in some sense'! Really the only thing wrong with what you say is the expression "in a queer way."

Typically, Wittgenstein's response to platonism is not, "What you're saying is *false,*" but rather, "What you say is all right; only there's nothing queer or magical about it." Wittgenstein doesn't deny that when I grasp the sense of a rule, the steps that I'm supposed to take are, in

---

3. The phrase is from *PI* II§i: "'Grief' describes a pattern which recurs, with different variations, in the weave of our life." I'll return to this remark in §5.3.

some sense, already present to my mind. (He doesn't think—as Wright thinks—that the question of which steps I'm supposed to take awaits determination by decision.) The platonist's problem is not that he wants to say that the steps are present, but that he imagines that *in* saying this, he's remarking on a mind-boggling fact.

Most of the platonist's words can be uttered innocently by someone who doesn't try to view signs apart from the applications that living beings make of them—apart, that is, from "the weave of our life." At *PI* §218, an interlocutor says, "The rule, once stamped with a particular meaning, traces the lines along which it is to be followed through the whole of space." An utterance of these words *might* be an expression of platonism, but it might be an innocent example of what Wittgenstein calls a "grammatical remark" about rules. Wittgenstein is not denying that rules reach out to their infinity of applications; he's urging us to free ourselves from a conception of what rules are in themselves according to which a rule's "reaching out to its applications" can be understood only as a sort of magical gulf-bridging.[4]

The responses to platonism that we find in Wright's and in Kripke's writing fail to address it at the right depth. The platonist's crucial mistake is one that he shares with both Kripke's sceptic and with Wright, namely, imagining that there's a gulf between every rule and its application. We overcome the impulse toward platonism only by coming to recognize this mistake as a mistake.

According to Wright and Wright's Wittgenstein, to say that a rule autonomously calls for this or that activity is to commit oneself to platonism. I've been arguing that this is not Wittgenstein's view. The platonist who figures in Wittgenstein's texts is someone who first imagines that there's a gulf between every rule and its application and only then thinks that somehow, mysteriously, the rule (or its meaning, or some-

---

4. McDowell suggests that "we can *always* frame threats of platonistic mythology, as they figure in Wittgenstein's landscape, on the pattern of *PI* §195." He continues: "The following is not a Wittgensteinian exchange, though on Wright's reading it ought to be: 'An intention determines what counts as conformity to it autonomously and independently of any subsequent judgements of its author'—'Platonism! Anathema!' The following is: 'An intention in some sense determines, in a *queer* way, what counts as conformity to it autonomously and independently of any subsequent judgements of its author.'—'But of course it does, "in *some* sense"! Really the only thing wrong with what you say is the expression "in a queer way"'" (McDowell 1998e, 54).

thing) autonomously manages to call for one activity rather than another. Once we stop thinking of words in isolation from the human lives in which they're embedded—once we give up imagining that there's a gulf between every rule and its application—we can say, innocently, that a particular rule autonomously called for this or that.[5]

*　　*　　*

"So what you're saying is that, while Wright's Wittgenstein thinks stipulation is what connects a rule with its correct applications, your Wittgenstein thinks it's 'the weave of our life'?"

5. We should not let the various ways in which the term "platonism" may be deployed obscure the crucial point here—that, according to Wittgenstein, someone might utter most of the platonist's words without falling into a conception of rules as mind-boggling. Indeed, although I won't speak this way, I would not object much to saying that what Wittgenstein is recommending is an innocent *kind* of platonism. In other words, we might grant Wright that *anyone* who affirms that a rule can autonomously call for one thing rather than another is to be called a "platonist" and then say that according to Wittgenstein there is a truistic, unmetaphysical kind of platonism which does not commit one to seeing rules (or their meanings) as mind-boggling. McDowell speaks this way about Wittgenstein and platonism in *Mind and World*. He distinguishes what he calls "naturalized platonism"—a position that he endorses and that he reads Wittgenstein as recommending—from a problematic kind of platonism that he calls "rampant platonism": "In rampant platonism, the rational structure within which meaning comes into view is independent of anything merely human, so that the capacity of our minds to resonate to it looks occult or magical. Naturalized platonism is platonistic in that the structure of the space of reasons has a sort of autonomy; it is not derivative from, or reflective of, truths about human beings that are capturable independently of having that structure in view. But this platonism is not rampant: the structure of the space of reasons is not constituted in splendid isolation from anything merely human" (McDowell 1996, 92). If I understand McDowell, his "rampant platonism" is what I have been referring to as "platonism," and what he calls "naturalized platonism" is close to the approach to these issues that I've been attributing to Wittgenstein.

McDowell is not the only commentator who characterizes Wittgenstein as an innocent sort of platonist. Writing about platonism in the philosophy of mathematics, W. W. Tait (1986) distinguishes between an "unintelligible" kind of platonism according to which there is a mathematical reality that is wholly "independent of our practice and which adjudicates its correctness" (361) and an innocent sort of platonism, which appears "not as a substantive philosophy or foundation of mathematics, but as a *truism*" (342). According to Tait, what Wittgenstein attacks is "a particular picture of Platonism" (348) and what he defends is a "version of Platonism" (348)—where this latter version of platonism is to be equated with "our ordinary conception of mathematics" (353).

The point is *not* that "the weave of our life" (or customs or institutions)[6]—rather than stipulation or interpretation—is what bridges the gulf between the statement of a rule and what would satisfy it. It would be better to say that when rules are seen as situated *within* our lives, it becomes apparent that such gulfs are exceptional. In general, *nothing* bridges a gulf between a rule and its application because no gulf opens up. It makes sense to speak of such a gulf only against a backdrop of cases in which there is no difficulty about what the statement of a rule means. *Sometimes,* I come upon an instruction that I don't understand. In such a situation, an interpretation might be what I need, but in general I need *nothing* of the sort. A philosopher who asks, "How is it that the statement of a rule is connected to its meaning?" has—even before she's offered any answer to the question—already succumbed to the idea that some link is needed if our words are to have significance; she presupposes that there is always a gulf between words and their meanings. Wittgenstein is not offering another account of the connection between words and their meanings. He is urging us to question our inclination to search for any such account: "If it is asked: 'How do sentences manage to represent?'—the answer might be: 'Don't you know? You certainly see it, when you use them.' For nothing is concealed" (*PI* §435).

*   *   *

In Kripke's presentation of the rule-following problematic, a sceptic challenges his interlocutor to cite facts about his former life that justify his current inclination to use the word "plus" in a particular way, i.e., to cite some fact that his meaning *plus* by "plus" might have consisted in. Wright claims that the best answer to Kripke's sceptic is "flat-

---

My reason for not wanting to say that Wittgenstein endorses an innocent kind of platonism is that this way of describing what he's up to is liable to give the impression that he is playing the same game as his interlocutors—that he is trying to explain what it is that links a rule with its applications. As will soon become clear, I take this to be a serious misreading of Wittgenstein's intentions.

6. At *PI* §199, Wittgenstein writes: "To obey a rule, to make a report, to give an order, to play a game of chess, are *customs* (uses, institutions)." One will misunderstand Wittgenstein if one takes passages such as this one to be offering an answer to a question like, "What bridges the gulf between a rule and what it requires?" (For a reading along these lines, see Bloor 1983.) Wittgenstein speaks of the customs and institutions in which our words have a life for the same reason that he speaks of the weave of our life—not to answer such questions, but to bring out what is wrong with them.

footed"—one that goes, *The fact about my past usage of "plus" that fixes it that I am now acting in accord with what I then meant by "plus" is just that I meant* plus *by "plus."* This answer has much to recommend it; it represents a refusal to accept the sceptic's implicit insistence that *something* must link a person's words with what he means by them. Wright fails, however, to do it justice. He *says* that the flat-footed response is correct, but in his attempt to explain how and why it can be correct, he winds up recommending a response that is anything but flat-footed: what fixes it that in the past I meant *plus* by "plus" is that I now judge that I meant *plus* by "plus." To Wright, the flat-footed answer to Kripke's sceptic *by itself* appears to avoid a genuine question—the question of what it is that "constitutes the truth of rule-informed judgment" (Wright 2001e, 211). But to understand Wittgenstein is to see that he thinks there is no real question here.

The point is not that Wright's words express a question that Wittgenstein thinks we must "quietistically" avoid. According to Wittgenstein, it is only when we conceive of words as cut off from the applications that living beings make of them that there even appears to be a question concerning how, in general, rule-informed judgments—e.g., the judgment that a particular recipe calls for the beating of egg whites—can be true. Freed from such a picture of words, we can meet a query like "What constitutes the truth of your judgment that the recipe calls for the beating of egg whites (rather than yolks or heavy cream)?" with a genuinely flat-footed response: "It *says* to beat egg whites. You can look for yourself."

4.2. Expression

I have been discussing Wittgenstein's views on the relation between words—e.g., the words in an order or a recipe—and their meanings. In the present section, I'll turn to what Wittgenstein has to say about a parallel relation, that between human behavior and the mental states and events that are expressed by it. Imagine that a chef gives an order to his assistant; he says, "Make a roux," whereupon she mixes flour and butter in a pan. Here, a philosopher might ask, "What fixes it that the chef's words require the assistant to mix fat and flour rather than, say, salt and molasses?" At this point, we know how Wittgenstein's various interlocutors would respond to this question. One would say that the chef's order requires that the assistant mix fat and flour thanks to the way in which it is *interpreted* (by the chef or by the chef and the assistant or by the language community or by whomever). Another, a platonist, would say that an item in (or somehow connected to) the chef's mind—one that can only be guessed at by the assistant—is what determines what he has asked her to do. A meaning sceptic would say that the chef's utterance doesn't really call for one bit of behavior any more than another. And a stipulativist would say that some sort of decision determines what the chef's order requires. Although these answers differ, they share a presupposition that might be put as follows: "Words are, in themselves, semantically inert—nothing more than dead noises or ink-marks. There is a gulf between every order and what it calls for." As we have seen, once we take it for granted that words are in this way dead, nothing—no interpretation or stipulation, for example—will seem to animate them satisfactorily. This does not mean that we ought to side with the sceptic and conclude that there are no facts about what our words mean. It is, Wittgenstein points out, only because we are led to consider words apart from their surroundings that we come to view them as divested of meaning in the first place. In a case like that of the chef and his assistant, a determinate order may be issued and understood without anyone's needing to interpret, guess, or stipulate anything. There is an innocent, nonplatonistic sense in which the chef's words are meaningful in themselves and a corresponding sense in which the assistant knows what she is required to do thanks to the fact that she heard what the chef said.

Now consider a related question that might be put as follows: "The chef's utterance expresses a *desire* that his assistant make a roux. What fixes it that the utterance expresses this mental state rather than some other?" This question differs from the one at issue in the preceding paragraph; this one concerns the chef's state of mind rather than the meaning of his utterance. Still, the answers that Wittgenstein's interlocutors would give are closely analogous to the ones canvassed above. The interlocutor who thinks that all signs require interpretation would say that the chef's utterance expresses one desire rather than another only under an interpretation. The platonist would say that the chef's utterance is associated with a hidden mental item—a desire—that can only be guessed at by his assistant. The sceptic would deny that the chef's utterance expresses one state of mind any more than another.

And the stipulativist would say that the chef's utterance expresses a determinate desire only thanks to someone's decision. All of these claims presuppose a view of human behavior that is analogous to the conception of signs according to which they are, in themselves, lifeless ink-marks or noises. The view might be put this way: "Our movements and their effects are, in themselves, without determinate *psychological* content. In order to understand how bodily movements may be expressive of a particular mental condition, we need to see what gives them psychological significance. If they are to be understood *as* psychologically significant, movements (such as those exhibited by the chef in our example) must somehow be *invested* with content (e.g., via interpretation)."

It is such a conception of human behavior, as mere bodily movement, that motivates Wright's constitutivism. Wright represents mental state self-attribution as a spring from which psychological content flows into human movements. But this is not Wittgenstein's view. Wittgenstein seeks to show that our activities seem to be divested of psychological content only if we view them apart from the contexts in which they appear—in isolation from "the weave of our life." It is because of the way that we look at pieces of behavior when we do philosophy (with blinders on, as it were) that we stop seeing the psychological depth in them. Returning to our example, just as we are able to recover our sense that the chef's words, when considered in context, just *are* meaningful, we need to see that it can be innocuous to say that the chef's behavior just *is* expressive of his desire. His assistant grasps what he wants her to do without the need for any sort of interpretation or stipulation. Wittgenstein can help us to return to the point where we no longer feel compelled to deny the platitude that, in ordinary circumstances, the chef's behavior makes his desire manifest.

*   *   *

Of course, desires are not the only inner states that are made manifest by our behavior. Nor is talking the only sort of activity that makes inner states manifest. Wittgenstein often calls attention to the way in which our facial expressions make a wide range of mental states visible to others:

> "We *see* emotion."—As opposed to what?—We do not see facial contortions and make inferences from them (like a doctor framing a diagno-

sis) to joy, grief, boredom. We describe a face immediately as sad, radi-
ant, bored, even when we are unable to give any other description to
the features.—Grief, one would like to say, is personified in the face.
(*Z*§225)

We do not, typically, need interpretations in order to understand a
person's facial expressions. Sometimes we do, when there is a real
doubt about what a facial expression means. (I might ask you what
your strange smile means.)[7] But it is a mistake to think that there is a
gulf between every facial expression and its psychological significance:
"It is possible to say 'I read timidity in this face' but at all events the
timidity does not seem to be merely associated, outwardly connected,
with the face; but fear is there, alive, in the features" (*PI*§537).[8]
Wright's constitutivism, like many other philosophical views of the relation between mind and body, depends upon the thought that our
movements must always be "outwardly connected" with their psychological significance. It is this thought that Wittgenstein seeks to
exorcise. If we start from the idea that all that is given to us in our experience of other people is psychologically neutral pieces of bodily behavior—movements which need to be somehow invested with psychological significance—we are left once again with a gulf either that
needs to be bridged (by, e.g., interpretation or stipulation) or that we
must conclude is unbridgeable (a conclusion that leads to scepticism
about other minds). But a smile is not a psychologically neutral bit of
behavior.

*   *   *

In *Z*§53, Wittgenstein writes:

> But how does the person in whom it goes on know which event the pro-
> cess is the expectation of? For he does not seem to be in uncertainty
> about it. It is not as if he observed a mental or other condition and
> formed a conjecture about its cause. He may well say: "I don't know
> whether it is only this expectation that makes me so uneasy today"; but
> he will not say: "I don't know whether this state of mind, in which I now
> am, is the expectation of an explosion or of something else."

7. See §§5.2–5.3 for a discussion of the sort of authority with which you might answer such a question.

8. Compare the use of "alive" in a passage we looked at earlier: "Every sign *by itself*
seems dead. *What* gives it life?—In use it is *alive*" (*PI* §432).

The statement "I am expecting a bang at any moment" is an *expression* of expectation. This verbal reaction is the movement of the pointer, which shows the object of expectation.

What does Wittgenstein mean when he says that the statement "I am expecting a bang at any moment" is an expression (rather than an observation report)? If we were to read Wittgenstein as a constitutivist, we might answer along the following lines: "An expectation is like a pointer in that it is, as it were, *aimed* at something—its object. Wittgenstein means to say that when I avow an expectation, I'm not reporting on the direction in which my mental state already points but, rather, setting the position of the pointer. When I say, 'I expect a bang,' I make it the case that *this* is what my expectation is directed toward." Now that we have seen that constitutivism has its roots in a picture of the connection between human behavior and psychology that Wittgenstein is trying to undermine, we have good reason to reject such a reading.

Let's instead consider the above passage alongside a section that comes a little later in *Zettel.* At §67, Wittgenstein writes:

> An expectation is embedded in a situation from which it takes its rise. The expectation of an explosion for example, may arise from a situation in which an explosion is *to be expected.* The man who expects it had heard two people whispering: "Tomorrow at ten o'clock the fuse will be lit." Then he thinks: perhaps someone means to blow up a house here. Towards ten o'clock he becomes uneasy, jumps at every sound, and at last answers the question why he is so tense: "I'm expecting. . . ." This answer will e.g. make his behaviour intelligible. It will enable us to fill out the picture of his thoughts and feelings.

To say that the man's self-ascription ("I'm expecting an explosion") makes it the case that he expects an explosion is to fail to appreciate the way in which his expectation is "embedded in a situation from which it takes its rise." If we consider only the fact that, as ten o'clock approaches, the man described in the passage is jumping at sounds—if we tear this one fact out of its context and ask what it signifies about his psychological condition—there will seem to be no clear answer. The behavior will seem empty, and we may be led to think that it must be the avowal of expectation that serves, as it were, to pour content into the man's empty movements.

Wittgenstein does not offer a theory about what gives our behavior, understood as empty movements, the significance that it has. Rather, he seeks to show that our puzzlement about the source of psychological content is due to the fact that in our theorizing we are led to divest human behavior of the context in which it makes sense. According to the constitutivist reading of Z§53, "the movement of the pointer" is what directs the person's expectation toward a particular sort of event. But notice that the last sentence of the passage does not say, "This verbal reaction is the movement of the pointer, which *determines* [or decides] the object of expectation." The sort of pointer that Wittgenstein has in mind is one that *shows* something, makes something manifest. An avowal of expectation is—like a smile or a wince—an expression of someone's psychological condition. Such an expression makes someone's expectation manifest.

4.3. Expressivism

Wright notes that there exists a "tradition of commentary" according to which Wittgenstein means to deny "that avowals are so much as *assertions*—that they make statements, true or false—proposing to view them rather as *expressions* of the relevant aspects of the subject's psychology" (Wright 1998, 34; 2001c, 359–360). He writes:

> Wittgenstein's famous suggestion in §244 is that we should see the avowal of pain as an acquired form of pain behaviour—something one learns to use to supplant or augment the natural expression of pain and which, the *expressivist* tradition of commentary suggests, is no more a *statement*—something with truth-evaluable content—than are such natural forms of expression.   (1998, 34)

Let's say, following Wright, that an "expressivist" commentary is one according to which Wittgenstein, in characterizing psychological self-ascriptions as expressions, means to be denying that they are truth-evaluable. According to this sort of reading, Wittgenstein holds that a typical avowal of pain expresses the speaker's pain but, like a wince, does not say anything either true or false.

So understood, Wittgenstein's position is open to a fairly obvious objection. David Rosenthal, who himself subscribes to an expressivist reading of Wittgenstein, states the objection as follows:

> In *Philosophical Investigations* Wittgenstein (1953) seems to have held, roughly, that although one can report that some other person is, for example, in pain, in one's own case one can only express the pain, and not report it as well. If so, sentences like 'I am in pain,' which ostensibly report bodily sensations, actually just express them.
>
> But however suggestive this idea may be, it is plainly possible to report explicitly that we are in such states. And it is indisputable that others sometimes assert of us that we are, or are not, in particular mental states, and we sometimes explicitly contradict what they say. It is not just that we undermine what they say, as I might by saying 'ouch' when you say I am not in pain. Rather, we literally deny what others say about us. If we were unable to report on our own states of mind, but could only express them, this direct denial of the ascriptions others make about us would be impossible. If you deny that I am in pain and I simply say 'ouch,' we have not thus far contradicted each other.   (Rosenthal 1993, 203)

Rosenthal reads Wittgenstein as proposing a rather extreme sort of expressivism: according to Rosenthal's Wittgenstein, it is not just unusual but impossible for someone with a headache to assert that she has one. As Wright notes, "the expressivist thesis about avowals can be merely that the typical use of such sentences is as expressions rather than assertions" (Wright 1998, 36; 2001c, 362). But I don't think the cogency of Rosenthal's objection depends on his having an extreme version of expressivism in view. If Wittgenstein held even that *typical* mental state avowals are not truth-evaluable, the objection would be warranted. Such avowals may indeed contradict—not merely undermine—what others say. Imagine that while suffering from a migraine, I wince and say to you, "My head really hurts a lot." Later, in an insecure moment, you accuse me of having lied about my condition in order to avoid spending the evening with you. Here, I might reply: "What I said was true. I had the worst headache I can remember." This is a very different conversation from any we might have had if the pain in my head had been expressed only nonlinguistically—if, e.g., I'd moaned, massaged my temples, and winced. In such a circumstance, you couldn't have accused me of *lying* about having had a headache—only of feigning one. And I would not have met such an accusation by saying that my moaning, wincing, and massaging were *true*.

Expressivism should be rejected. But as I read Wittgenstein, he is no expressivist; his position is not vulnerable to the sort of objection that Rosenthal raises. While Wittgenstein does say that mental state avowals are expressions, he does not deny that they are truth-evaluable. The influence of the expressivist reading is based, to a large extent, on an assumption that has no real foothold in Wittgenstein's writings, an assumption that could be stated as follows: "A given speech act might describe the speaker's state of mind—i.e., assert what state of mind she is in—*or* it might express her state of mind. But it can't do both these things. Expressing and asserting are, in a way, mutually exclusive." A commitment to this assumption (whose prevalence is probably due in large part to the influence of emotivism in ethics)[9] is manifest in Rosenthal's own views about mental state avowals. According to Rosenthal:

> I can communicate my suspicion that the door is open either by expressing my suspicion or by explicitly telling you about it. . . .
>
> . . . In saying I suspect something[,] I report, rather than express, my suspicion.   (Rosenthal 1993, 200)

Is this right? Imagine that I suspect something and say so: I say, "I'm beginning to suspect that my Uncle Jack has been embezzling funds from our company." After saying this, could I rightly be described as never having expressed a suspicion that my uncle was embezzling funds? *Pace* Rosenthal, typically, when I assert that I harbor a suspicion, I *thereby* express the suspicion. This point is made by Alston (1967):

9. Emotivists are moved to claim that moral statements are expressions by a conviction that there are no moral facts for moral statements to be true to. (See, e.g., Ayer 1946, 107–109.) In claiming that an utterance of "That's morally wrong" is an expression, the emotivist avoids seeing it as an attempt to utter a truth. Expressions, after all, *need* not be assertions. But it's one thing to say that expressions need not be assertions and quite another to say that they *cannot* be. If someone sincerely asserts, e.g., that the Yankees will win the World Series, he expresses his opinion that the Yankees will win the World Series. And, according to Wittgenstein, when someone asserts that he is in pain, he is likely to be expressing (not an *opinion* that he's in pain, but) his pain.

I can express my enthusiasm for your plan just as well by saying 'I'm very enthusiastic about your plan', as I can by saying 'What a tremendous plan!', 'Wonderful', or 'Great!' I can express disgust at X just as well by saying 'I'm disgusted', as by saying 'How revolting!', or 'Ugh'. I can express approval as well by saying 'I completely approve of what you are doing' as I can by saying 'Swell', or 'Good show'. And I can express annoyance as well by saying 'That annoys me no end' as by saying 'Damn'.

This shows that expressing and asserting are not mutually exclusive in the way commonly supposed.   (16)

Once we reject the assumption that expressing and asserting are "mutually exclusive in the way commonly supposed," expressivist commentaries on Wittgenstein lose much of their *prima facie* appeal. Wittgenstein does indicate that we should think of mental state avowals as, typically, expressions, but this does not commit him to holding that such utterances are not truth-evaluable.

A commentator who reads Wittgenstein as an expressivist might appeal for support to passages such as the one that follows—passages suggesting that, typically, mental state avowals are expressions *rather than reports:* "When someone says 'I hope he'll come'—is this a *report* [*Bericht*] about his state of mind, or an *expression* [*Äußerung*] of his hope?—I can, for example, say it to myself. And surely I am not giving myself a report" (*PI* §585).[10] Doesn't this show that according to Wittgenstein, an avowal of hope is typically an expression *and not* an assertion? Well, we need to ask the following question: When Wittgenstein indicates that some mental state avowal is not a *report*, does he mean that it should be understood as lacking a truth-value? The above-cited passages from Rosenthal suggest as much. When Rosenthal writes that, according to Wittgenstein, "in one's own case one can only express the pain, and not report it as well," he means to be denying, on Wittgenstein's behalf, that pain avowals are truth-evaluable. But Wittgenstein doesn't use "report" in this way. If he did, *PI* §585 (the passage just cited) would be quite puzzling. Why would he suppose it to be *obvious* ("And surely . . .") that I cannot say something true to myself? We'll un-

10. Where Wittgenstein uses the word "Äußerung," Anscombe's translations sometimes gives us "expression" and sometimes "manifestation." In this passage, I've departed from her translation, changing "manifestation" to "expression."

derstand Wittgenstein better if we gloss his use of "report" as follows: *an attempt (or merely apparent attempt)[11] to inform someone of a fact that the speaker has learned or ascertained.* Given this gloss, the final sentence of the quote from §585 doesn't look so puzzling. But notice that given this gloss, it doesn't follow from an avowal's not being a report that it lacks a truth-value. An avowal of hope that is not a report may yet be a true assertion.

In *Zettel,* Wittgenstein sets down what he calls a "Plan for the treatment of psychological concepts" that begins as follows:

> Psychological verbs characterized by the fact that the third person of the present is to be verified by observation, the first person not.
>
> Sentences in the third person of the present: information. In the first person present: expression. ((Not quite right.))
>
> The first person of the present akin to an expression. (*Z*§472; *RPP2* §63)

As we have seen, Wittgenstein will often say of a mental state avowal that it *is* an expression. Why, then, does he indicate here that to say this isn't "quite right"? I want to suggest that when Wittgenstein says it is "Not quite right" to assimilate psychological self-ascriptions to expressions, he is, in effect, rejecting expressivism. These utterances aren't *exactly* like facial and bodily expressions: there is a crucial difference, viz., that they have an assertoric dimension; they may be true or false. Still, psychological self-ascriptions are akin to facial expressions; typically, they make our mental states manifest in the way that facial expressions do. In the end, it is not particularly important whether we say that psychological self-ascriptions *are* expressions or that they are *akin* to them, as long as we keep in view both how they are like winces and smiles and how they are unlike them. The expressivist loses her grip on the latter. As I read Wittgenstein, he does not.

*   *   *

As long as we take it for granted that, according to Wittgenstein, an avowal of, e.g., pain cannot both express a pain and say something true, we seem to be faced with a dilemma. On one horn, we read Wittgenstein as an expressivist and so characterize his position as open

---

11. A report may, after all, be a lie.

to fairly easy refutation. This horn is grasped by Rosenthal as well as, e.g., Robert Fogelin (1987). The latter discusses and defends an objection to Wittgenstein that he imagines being stated as follows:

> "When I say that I have a pain in my foot, I am saying something about my foot, namely, that I have a pain in it. Of course this is different from saying that I have an artery in my foot or, even, that I have a wound in my foot. These are different kinds of assertions with different kinds of verification procedures, etc., but surely they are all assertions (reports, descriptions) about my foot!!"   (Fogelin 1987, 197)

On the other horn—if we don't wish to saddle Wittgenstein with a view quite so easily refuted—we can try to ignore or minimize the significance of his oft-repeated suggestion that psychological self-ascriptions be understood as expressions. Both Wright and McDowell grasp this horn. When Wright speaks about Wittgenstein on first-person authority, he typically says nothing about expression.[12] As for McDowell, I know of only one place in his writing where he remarks on a suggestion by Wittgenstein that we think of mental state avowals as expressing their subject matter. In *Mind and World,* immediately after he has first set out the middle path account of sensations, he writes:

> This is a very difficult area. Wittgenstein himself sometimes seems to betray an understandable wish to duck the difficulties. What I have in mind here is the fact that he sometimes seems to toy with denying that self-ascriptions of sensation are assertions, articulations of judgements about states of affairs, at all.   (1996, 22)

There is a footnote at this point that reads as follows:

> For instance, p. 68 of *The Blue Book* . . . : "The difference between the propositions 'I have pain' and 'he has pain' is not that of 'L. W. has pain' and 'Smith has pain.' Rather it corresponds to the difference between moaning and saying that someone moans." I would not dispute what is said in the first of these sentences. But sentences like the sec-

12. Wright (1998, 2001c) does mention expression, but only in the context of rejecting the emphasis placed on it by expressivist commentaries. And there is a sentence in Wright 2001d that mentions Wittgenstein's suggestion that "avowals are a form of *expression*" (443)—but, here too, it looks as though Wright thinks we should be careful not to accord this suggestion too much significance.

ond have suggested, at least to some commentators, a doctrine that assimilates "avowals" to other modes of expression, so as to distance them from assertions, and that strikes me as a cop-out.

Now, I don't quite disagree with what McDowell says in this footnote. It *is* a mistake to read Wittgenstein as claiming that mental state avowals are expressions *rather than* assertions. But McDowell's point doesn't seem to be that Wittgenstein thinks there is an assertoric *as well as* an expressive dimension to mental state avowals. (After the note about copping out, the idea that mental state avowals might express their subject matter doesn't surface again.) He seems to think that we must either read Wittgenstein as copping out—as denying that an avowal of pain is an assertion—or ignore the fact that Wittgenstein seems to want to say that such avowals are expressions of pain.

Rosenthal, Fogelin, Wright, and McDowell—all of them—are right to reject the thesis that mental state avowals are expressions rather than assertions. But they are wrong to assume that if we take seriously the many passages in which Wittgenstein says that avowals of pain, expectation, hope, and the rest are expressions, we must saddle him with this thesis. To maintain that some utterance functions as an expression is not—or, anyway, need not be—to deny that it is an assertion. One of my goals in this chapter has been to point to a better way of understanding what Wittgenstein means when he suggests that an avowal of pain, hope, or expectation is, or is akin to, an expression. In Chapter 5, I'll try to show how this suggestion of Wittgenstein's can help us to make sense of both first-person authority and consciousness.

Authority and Consciousness

Two morals of the preceding chapter could be put as follows: First, it's a mistake to think of what is given in our experience of other people's behavior as mere sound and movement divested of psychological import. An expression of pain or hope can make someone's psychological state manifest to others. And second, one of the ways in which we express our psychological states is by ascribing them to ourselves in words. A person may express, e.g., his intention to read *Middlemarch* by asserting that this is something he intends to do.

In the section that follows, I'll show that these morals yield a short explanation of the authority with which we speak about our own mental states. In §§5.2–5.3, I'll flesh out this explanation in order to account for two kinds of first-person authority that we haven't yet discussed. And in §§5.4–5.5, I'll suggest a related account of what it is that distinguishes conscious mental states from unconscious ones.

5.1. A Three-Paragraph Account of First-Person Authority

At the start of Chapter 1, I characterized the phenomenon of first-person authority as follows: "If you want to know what I think, feel, imagine, or intend, I am a good person—indeed, usually the best person—to ask." Shortly thereafter, another feature of this sort of authority came to light: Psychological self-ascriptions don't often appear to be based on behavioral evidence. I am, as a rule, entitled to avow beliefs, fears, sensations, etc. even when I'm unable to cite evidence in support of the avowal. At this point, we are in a position to consider a very brief explanation of these facts—a three-paragraph account of first-person authority—that is suggested by the two morals just drawn from Chapter 4. So:

(1) If you want to know my psychological condition, I'm usually the best person to ask, for just the same reason that my face is the best one to look at. My mental state self-ascriptions often express, and so make manifest, that which they are ascriptions of. Attention to them, like attention to my facial expressions, puts you in a position to perceive my psychological condition. Of course, you might learn, e.g., that I'm in pain from someone other than me—a mutual friend, perhaps—from what she says about me, or even from *her* facial expression. But were this to occur, you would learn something about my psychological condition at second hand, not by seeing for yourself. Such a case would stand in contrast to one in which you learn that I am in pain by seeing the suffering in my face or by hearing it in my avowal of pain. In the latter sort of case, your assessment of my state of mind would not depend on anyone else's discernment, not even mine.

(2) Why is it that I seem to require no behavioral evidence when I avow, e.g., that I'm afraid? No evidence is called for when I smile or wince either. Mental state self-ascriptions are not, typically, reports. They require no more evidence than do smiles. When I say, "My head hurts," I'm not remarking on a fact that I have learned on this or that basis, e.g., via observation or inference.

(3) If mental state self-ascriptions are so like facial expressions, why does there seem to be a philosophical problem having to do with the authority that attaches to the former, but not the latter? Well, we're not inclined to speak of the *authority* of smiles at all, and this is due to a difference between smiles and avowals of happiness. A smile expresses a state of mind without saying anything either true or false. But an avowal of happiness typically performs two functions: it expresses the speaker's happiness, and it says something true—that the speaker is happy. Unlike a smile or a wince, an avowal of happiness has an assertoric function. This is why—although you should attend both to my facial expressions and to what I say about myself, if you wish to learn my state of mind—we speak of *authority* only in connection with what I say about myself. Or, rather, *philosophers* speak of authority in connection with what I say about myself; "first-person authority" is, after all, a bit of

philosophers' jargon. Now, it's not *wrong* to say that we speak with a special authority about our own states of mind. But the word "authority" is liable to mislead us—to lead us to assimilate a mental state self-ascription to some other kind of statement that we think of as coming with special authority, e.g., that of an eye-witness or of an army colonel who declares an area off-limits. It is only when we take note of the way in which mental state self-ascriptions are akin to smiles and winces that first-person authority can come into focus as an unsurprising concomitant of the fact that one of the ways in which a person may express her state of mind is by commenting on it.

5.2. Other Varieties of First-Person Authority

How satisfied should we be with the three-paragraph account of first-person authority? Perhaps not very, just yet. In what follows, I'll raise an objection to it, one that exploits the fact that there are kinds of first-person authority that we have not yet considered.

Imagine the following scenario:

> Franny and Zooey are sitting in a restaurant, drinking coffee and talking. After complaining of a headache, Franny rummages through her pockets looking for an aspirin. While she is thus engaged, Zooey makes a lame joke about the watery coffee that the two of them have been drinking. Franny groans audibly, whereupon Zooey asks: "What did that mean? Did you groan because your head hurts, or didn't you like my joke?" Franny answers unhesitatingly, decisively, and apparently without epistemic grounds, "Neither. I groaned because of how much I detest this coffee."[1]

This story illustrates that we speak with a kind of first-person authority not only about our mental states, but also about our behavior. In answer to Zooey's question, Franny says more than that she detests her coffee; she says something about her groan. Zooey might well have been aware that Franny detested the coffee before he asked her why she'd groaned. Nonetheless, in answering his question, Franny tells

---

1. Compare the example set out in *PI*§§666 and 682. By the way, I think Wittgenstein's best remarks about this example and others like it are to be found in the first few pages of *Zettel* rather than in the *Investigations*. (See especially *Z*§§16 and 19.)

him something that he did not already know—that her behavior was an expression (not of the pain in her head, nor of her opinion of his joke, but) of her distaste for her coffee.

Imagine that the story continues as follows:

> Franny finds an aspirin and swallows it, thinking to herself, "It's not just my head; my *back* hurts too. These chairs are awful." Having already complained about her headache and her coffee, she decides not to mention her backache to Zooey.

Here Franny could be said to think, rather than speak, with first-person authority. She ascribes a pain to herself with ease, accuracy, and no apparent basis in behavioral evidence—just as if she were speaking aloud. But she does not speak aloud; she does not make the pain in her back manifest to Zooey. We could say that she avows it to herself, in thought. Not only do we speak with first-person authority about both our mental states and our behavior; we *think* with a kind of first-person authority too.

A bit of reflection on this conclusion might lead someone to argue against the three-paragraph account of first-person authority as follows: "According to the three-paragraph account, what explains the authority with which we speak about our own mental states is the fact that, typically, mental state avowals express their subject matter. This feature of avowals cannot help us to make sense of either the authority with which we speak about our own behavior or that with which we ascribe mental states to ourselves in thought. When Franny thinks, 'My back hurts,' she does not express the pain in her back. And when she says, 'I groaned because of how much I detest this coffee,' she does not express her groan (or rather, it makes no sense to describe someone as 'expressing a groan'). Of course, ideally, we would like to understand all these phenomena, so the three-paragraph account is, perhaps, a bit disappointing on this score. But the real problem with it is this: it seems implausible that the account can be getting things right about the kind of authority that it is meant to explain, given that it sheds no light on the other kinds. (Surely, once we understand why behavioral evidence seems irrelevant to a spoken self-ascription of pain, we should also understand, or be close to understanding, why such evidence seems irrelevant to a self-ascription in thought.) We should therefore reject—or, anyway, remain unconvinced by—the three-paragraph account and seek an explanation of first-person authority that does not make so much of the fact that some of our statements express their subject matter."[2]

In the next section, I'll answer this objection; I'll defend the three-paragraph account through an examination of, first, the authority with which we speak about our own behavior and, then, the authority with which we ascribe mental states to ourselves in thought. I'll argue that the three-paragraph account of (one kind of) first-person authority does, after all, constitute a first step toward a more general explanation of the various kinds of first-person authority that have now come into view.

5.3. Expression and Context

> In a concrete case I can indeed ask "Why did I say that, what did I mean by it?"—and I might answer the question too; but not on the ground of observing what accompanied the speaking. And my answer would supplement, paraphrase, the earlier utterance.   (*PI* II§ix)

> My own relation to my words is wholly different from other people's. (*PI* II§x)

> [H]ow a sentence is meant can be expressed by an expansion of it . . . (*OC* §349)

What accounts for the authority with which Franny speaks about her groan? And how is this sort of authority connected to that with which she speaks when she comments only on her own mental condition, not on her behavior as well?

We can begin to address these questions by considering a related case that is a bit easier to come to terms with. Imagine a corporate board meeting at which the chief executive officer has this to say about a midlevel employee: "Phillips is a real team-player, by which I mean—not that he's a stupid sheep, but—that he won't help himself at the expense of this company." We might ask: How did the CEO learn what

---

2. Crispin Wright takes the fact that "the content of an avowal is always available to figure just in a subject's thoughts, without public expression" as a demonstration of "the unplayability of the expressivist position" concerning first-person authority (Wright 1998, 38; 2001c, 364). (See §4.3 for a discussion of "expressivism" and its relation to the position that I'm defending.)

she meant by "team-player"? Did she listen to the first half of her sentence and interpret it? If so, why do the other board members attach such weight to *her* interpretation of the remark?

These questions are confused. The confusion could be characterized as follows: the CEO didn't need to *learn* what she meant; the second half of her sentence is not a report on the first half but rather an expression of its meaning. But now, what does *this* mean? Part of what it means is that the members of the board hear the *whole* sentence and understand it as a coherent unit; the two halves of the sentence make sense in light of each other. The second half of the CEO's sentence is as much a part of her assessment of Phillips as is the first. To understand what the whole sentence means, to hear what the CEO is saying about Phillips, a listener needs to take in the second half of the sentence together with the first. We can call the second half of the sentence a gloss on, or interpretation of, the first, but it isn't *merely* an interpretation; it's an elaboration, a fleshing out. It makes the meaning of the first half manifest in a way that someone else's interpretation would not. The weight that the board members accord the second half of her sentence reflects the fact that a sentence is what we might call a unit of intelligibility. The word "team-player" and the CEO's gloss on it are two parts of a single, coherent, intelligible whole.

Consider a variation on our story: At the board meeting, the CEO says, "Phillips is a real team-player," without elaborating on what she means by this. Five years later, her secretary is reading through the minutes of the meeting. He asks her what she meant by "team-player." The CEO remembers neither the meeting nor Phillips. She says, "Well, that's not a word that I often use. I suppose I might have meant it ironically, as a kind of insult to this Phillips." The CEO interprets her own remark as if it were made by someone else; she takes up a third-person perspective on it. Her two remarks, separated by years and forgetting, don't constitute a single unit of intelligibility. The second remark might provide information (or misinformation) about the first, but what we have in this version of the story are two separate remarks, not two parts of something that make sense together. In this version of the story, the CEO's second remark doesn't come with the sort of authority that we saw in the first version. Here, she is not, in the same way, expressing her meaning; she's merely interpreting something that she once said.

*   *   *

In the introduction to *The Foundations of Arithmetic*, Frege writes, "In the enquiry that follows, I have kept to three fundamental principles." The second of these principles is "never to ask for the meaning of a word in isolation, but only in the context of a proposition" (Frege 1953, x). Later in the book, he writes, "It is enough if the proposition taken as a whole has a sense; it is this that confers on the parts also their content" (71). Frege's context principle constitutes a rejection of the view that understanding a sentence requires one to grasp the meanings of independently intelligible sentence-parts. For Frege, the sentence is the primary unit of intelligibility. A word has the meaning that it does only in the context of a sentence.

An example of Frege's helps to make the point. Compare the following sentences:

(1) Vienna is the capital of Austria.
(2) Trieste is no Vienna.

The logical role of the word "Vienna" is different in these sentences. In the first sentence, it functions as a proper name. In the second, it functions, Frege says, as "a concept-word, like 'metropolis'" (Frege 1952, 50). It would make sense to say, "Although Trieste is no Vienna, Paris *is* a Vienna—the only one in France." Imagine that someone who said this also had occasion to say, "Vienna is the capital of Austria." She would not thereby commit herself to the view that the capital of Austria is in France. The word "Vienna" does not mean the same thing in sentences (1) and (2). We come to see what a particular use of a word means only when we consider it in the context of a whole sentence.

I want to suggest that what goes for the word "Vienna" also goes for the word "team-player" in the CEO example: it means what it does only in the context of the whole in which it appears. But in the sentence uttered by the CEO ("Phillips is a real team-player, by which I mean—not that he's a stupid sheep, but—that he won't help himself at the expense of this company"), we see a special kind of sentential context, one that constitutes a gloss on, or interpretation of, that which it contextualizes. In the sentence "Trieste is no Vienna," the words "Trieste is no" contextualize the word "Vienna," but they do not constitute an interpretation of it. We could say that the CEO speaks with a special authority concerning what she meant by the word "team-player" because she is offering an interpretation of it that is not a *mere* interpretation. Her interpretation contextualizes that which it interprets in a way that an interpretation offered by one of the other board members would not.

*   *   *

One can hear echoes of Frege's context principle in both the *Tractatus* and the *Investigations*. At *Tractatus* 3.3, Wittgenstein says: "[O]nly in the context of a sentence has a name meaning" (1922). And in §49 of the *Investigations,* he writes: "We may say: *nothing* has so far been done, when a thing has been named. It has not even *got* a name except in a language-game. This was what Frege meant too, when he said that a word had a meaning only as part of a sentence." Wittgenstein doesn't merely inherit Frege's principle; he reshapes it in a number of ways, two of which I'll call to your attention. One of them is signaled by Wittgenstein's use of the term "language-game" in this passage from the *Investigations.* He speaks of language-games where Frege spoke of sentences. However it is that one ought precisely to characterize what Wittgenstein means by "language-game," it is clear that language-games are, so to speak, *wider* than sentences. Frege's point—that our words mean what they do only in their contexts of use—is still present in the *Investigations,* but Wittgenstein seems to have wider contexts in mind. Consider the following passages:

> "After he had said this, he left her as he did the day before."—Do I understand this sentence? Do I understand it just as I should if I heard it in the course of a narrative? If it were set down in isolation I should say, I don't know what it's about.   (*PI* §525)

> The phrase "description of a state of mind" characterizes a certain *game.* And if I just hear the words "I am afraid" I might be able to *guess* which game is being played here (say on the basis of the tone), but I won't really know it until I am aware of the context.   (*LWPP1* §50)

About the first of these passages, I want to say that there's a sense in which I *do* understand the sentence mentioned, but—and this is Wittgenstein's point—there is another sense in which I don't understand it at all. I have no idea whom the sentence is about or what condition "he" left "her" in the day before. The second passage makes a similar point. What someone is doing when he utters the words "I am afraid" depends on a context that is wider than a sentence. Wittgenstein wants to show that the functions and meanings that our words have depend on the ways in which they are situated not just in sentences, but in conversations and stories; in stretches of discourse, thought, and behavior; in spans of human life. We could say that he reshapes Frege's context principle by enlarging the contexts of use to which it, or some descendant of it, applies.[3]

Here, we might consider another variation on the CEO example: Imagine that the CEO says, "Phillips is a real team-player," without glossing what she means by this. Later in the meeting, one of the board members says to her, "A few minutes ago, you remarked that Phillips is a team-player. I wasn't sure just how you meant that. Were you implying that he's not particularly creative or original?" The CEO replies, "No; I meant that he's good at getting along with people." In this example, the CEO's initial remark about Phillips and her gloss on it are not part of a single sentence. They are, however, part of what we can think of as a somewhat broader and looser unit of intelligibility— one comprising the CEO's remarks about Phillips at the board meeting. The CEO speaks with authority here too, but perhaps not quite the same degree of authority as in the original example. The contextual connection between "team-player" and her gloss on it is not so tight here as in the first version of the story;[4] there is a bit more room to question whether she might be concealing, or mistaken about, what she meant.

3. I don't mean to suggest that Frege thinks a single sentence, floating free of any language, would have a meaning. The meaning of a sentence (and so of its subsentential parts) depends, for Frege, on the inferential relations it would bear to other sentences that might be produced in the language. So there's a sense in which Frege does have a very wide context in mind—the context of the whole language. And it might very well be misleading to say, e.g., "Frege takes only the sentential context of a word to bear on its meaning, while Wittgenstein considers contexts that are wider than sentences." The point I'm making in the text has to do with the relation between the meaning of a particular word or string of words as produced by a speaker and what the speaker says (or what he and his conversation partners say) before and after the string. About such contexts, we *can* say, Wittgenstein has wider ones in mind than does Frege.

4. I'm not suggesting that a single sentence always constitutes a tighter unit of intelligibility than a stretch of sentences. There would be no significant difference between the first version of the story and one in which the CEO uttered the following *pair* of sentences: "Phillips is a real team-player. By this I mean—not that he's a stupid sheep, but—that he won't help himself at the expense of this company."

So one way in which Wittgenstein reshapes and extends Frege's context principle is by calling attention to contexts of use that are wider than sentences. And now, a second way he does this is by bringing out that it is not only linguistic items—words or sentences—that depend for their significance on their surroundings. The following passage concerns the significance of a wordless activity, the placing of a crown on someone's head:

> A coronation is the picture of pomp and dignity. Cut one minute of this proceeding out of its surroundings: the crown is being placed on the head of the king in his coronation robes.—But in different surroundings gold is the cheapest of metals, its gleam is thought vulgar. There the fabric of the robe is cheap to produce. A crown is a parody of a respectable hat. And so on. (*PI* §584)

In thinking about such examples, it helps to imagine glimpsing a few seconds out of a movie. Suppose that while channel-surfing, you catch a moment of film in which a man, whose face you cannot see, is slowly closing a door. There is a sense in which you know what you are seeing—a man closing a door—but another sense in which you don't. You don't know the meaning of this activity, this door-closing, because you don't know how it figures in the story. Perhaps if you saw more of the film, you would want to say that in closing the door, the man was breaking off a love affair, or trying to stay hidden, or insulting the butler. The significance of our activities, both with and without words, depends on how they are situated in our lives.

*   *   *

I opened this section by raising two questions: What accounts for the authority with which Franny speaks about her groan? And how is this sort of authority related to that with which she speaks when she comments only on her own mental state? We are now in a position to answer the first of these questions. Franny's gloss on her groan is a close cousin to the CEO's authoritative gloss on her use of the word "team-player." When Franny says, "I groaned because of how much I detest this coffee," she doesn't merely interpret her own behavior. Her groan and her interpretation of it make sense together, in light of each other. They function together to express Franny's dissatisfaction with her coffee. Someone else might offer an interpretation of Franny's groan, but it would not contribute to the expression of Franny's distaste; it would not share in the expressive labor. Franny's interpretation fleshes out her groan in much the same way that the second half of the CEO's sentence fleshes out the first. This is why someone who wishes to understand her groan—to learn what it expresses—should pay special attention to *her* interpretation of it. Like the CEO's authority, Franny's derives from the fact that her interpretation contextualizes the very thing that it is an interpretation of.

By the way, this kind of authority, the authority with which a person says what it is that her own behavior expresses, plays an important role in our lives. When I state the beliefs and desires that moved me to this or that *action*—when I answer the question "Why did you do that?"—I (usually) exhibit this kind of authority. Instead of focusing on Franny's interpretation of a groan, we could have taken the following as our point of departure:

> Franny reaches across to Zooey's side of the table in the direction of the cream, the sugar, and a book that the two of them have been discussing. Zooey says, "What are you reaching for? I'll hand it to you." Franny replies, "The cream."

Here Franny interprets her own action—her reaching across the table. But her interpretation isn't a *mere* interpretation; it works *with* the action to express her desire for cream. She speaks with authority (not because she has the best view of her own behavior, but) because her interpretation contextualizes, in this way, the very action that it's an interpretation of.

*   *   *

According to Wittgenstein, it is not only our words and activities whose significance depends on the "manifestations of life" that surround them; so too do our states of mind. In the section of the *Investigations* that immediately precedes the coronation passage, Wittgenstein writes: "Could someone have a feeling of ardent love or hope for the space of one second—*no matter what* preceded or followed this second?—What is happening now has significance—in these surroundings. The surroundings give it its importance" (*PI* §583). Frege says "never to ask for the meaning of a word in isolation, but only in the context of a proposition." Wittgenstein might have said never to ask after someone's mental condition in isolation, but only in the context of the events of his life:

> "Grief" describes a pattern which recurs, with different variations, in the weave of our life. If a man's bodily expression of sorrow and of joy alternated, say with the ticking of a clock, here we should not have the characteristic formation of the pattern of sorrow or of the pattern of joy.
>
> "For a second he felt violent pain."—Why does it sound queer to say: "For a second he felt deep grief"? Only because it so seldom happens?
>
> But don't you feel grief *now*? ("But are you playing chess *now*?") (*PI* II§i)

A person *can* feel grief at a particular moment. But that it is *grief* he feels has to do with what comes before and after that moment. This is not to say that someone's grieving at time *t2 makes it the case* that he was grieving at *t1* (any more than it is to say that what a person does at *t1* makes it the case that he's grieving at *t2*). But we *can* say that at each moment, a person's psychological condition makes sense in light of feelings, behavior, and events that precede and succeed it.

We can now address the second question that was raised at the opening of this section: what is the connection between the sort of authority with which Franny speaks about her own behavior (when she says "I groaned because of how much I detest this coffee") and that which accompanies psychological self-ascriptions that make no reference to behavior? Just as Franny's interpretation of her own behavior contextualizes that which it interprets and so isn't a mere interpretation, our psychological self-ascriptions contextualize that which they ascribe and so aren't mere ascriptions. When someone ascribes, e.g., an expectation to himself, the ascription is a part of the situation in which the expectation participates and from which it, as it were, draws its life. An avowal of expectation bears a relation to a person's psychological condition that is, in this respect, like the relation that Franny's gloss on her groan bears to the groan itself.

I am, in effect, suggesting that we understand the relation between a mental state and its expression as a species of a broader genus. Franny's groan expresses her distaste. Although her interpretation of the groan cannot be said to "express her groan," still, the relation between the interpretation and the groan is akin to that between the groan and the distaste. In each case, we have two items that make sense together, in light of each other, in something like the way that the parts of a sentence make sense together.

*　　*　　*

Recall the objection to the three-paragraph account of first-person authority that was stated in §5.2. It hinged on the fact that we seem to exhibit a kind of first-person authority not only (1) when we speak directly about our states of mind, but also (2) when we speak about what's expressed by our behavior and (3) when we merely ascribe mental states to ourselves in thought. Thus far, I have been trying to elucidate the connection between (1) and (2). Let us now turn to (3). And let's stay with our example: Franny thinks, but does not say, "My back hurts." What explains the authority that might be said to attend this thought? And what's the connection between it and the other kinds of first-person authority that we have been discussing?

Wittgenstein notes that when a child learns to talk, "the verbal expression of pain replaces crying" (*PI* §244). As we mature, another such replacement occurs: we learn merely to *think*, rather than say aloud, "That hurts." Now, perhaps it would sound odd to use the word "expression" to refer to such a thought. But nothing very important hinges on this. The important point is that when we learn to substitute *either* the spoken *or* the merely thought self-ascription for the cry, things don't suddenly turn perceptual or evidential; a true self-ascription of either sort needn't be based on observation or evidence any more than a cry of pain is. Regardless of whether a mental state self-ascription in thought is naturally called an "expression," such ascriptions are akin to expressions in this sense.

For my part, I do find it natural to use the word "expression" to refer even to thoughts. Imagine a man who is trying to tiptoe into bed so as not to disturb his sleeping wife. While thus engaged, he stubs a toe on one of the bed's metal legs. He feels the impulse to cry out but suppresses it and only thinks, "Ow, ow, ow, ow, ow; that *really* hurts." I'd call this thought an expression of pain. Granted, it's not a bit of public behavior, but dreams, which are not bits of public behavior, are often said to express wishes or fears.

Wittgenstein writes:

> An expectation is embedded in a situation from which it takes its rise. The expectation of an explosion for example, may arise from a situation in which an explosion is *to be expected*. The man who expects it had heard two people whispering: "Tomorrow at ten o'clock the fuse will be lit." Then he thinks: perhaps someone means to blow up a house here. Towards ten o'clock he becomes uneasy, jumps at every sound, and at last answers the question why he is so tense: "I'm expecting. . . ." This answer will e.g. make his behaviour intelligible. It will enable us to fill out the picture of his thoughts and feelings.   (*Z* §67; this passage was discussed briefly in §4.2)

The man's expectation is "embedded in a situation" in something like the way that a word's meaning is embedded in the context of a sentence or a paragraph. Notice that this "situation" includes not only the man's *saying*, "I expect an explosion," but also his *thinking*, "Perhaps someone means to blow up a house here." This thought, like the man's spoken avowal, helps contextualize his expectation. I am claiming that an expectation and the ascription of it to oneself make sense together, in light of each other, regardless of whether the latter is spoken aloud or merely thought. Thus, whether I am (1) avowing a pain aloud, (2) ascribing a pain to myself in thought, or (3) stating that some gesture or grimace of mine was an expression of pain, my self-ascription (or interpretation) is not *mere* ascription (or interpretation); it contextualizes that which it ascribes (or interprets).

According to the three-paragraph account of first-person authority, I speak with a special sort of authority about my own mental states because mental state avowals express their subject matter. My aim in the present section has been to shed sufficient light on what it means to say that a mental state avowal expresses its subject matter in order for us to see other sorts of self-ascription as doing similar work and so not be bothered by the fact that these ascriptions come with a similar sort of authority. A person who merely thinks, "My back hurts"—who ascribes pain to herself in thought—may be understood as expressing her pain or, anyway, as doing something akin to expressing it. And even though we don't speak of "expressing a groan," when Franny says, "I was groaning because of how much I detest this coffee," her utterance bears a relation to her behavior that is also like the relation a wince bears to a pain. Both the authority with which we speak about our own behavior and that with which we merely think about our own states of mind can be understood along the lines laid down by the three-paragraph account.

5.4. Conscious or Unconscious

> Yes, I preferred the elderly and discontented doctor, surrounded by friends and cherishing honest hopes; and bade a farewell to the liberty, the comparative youth, the light step, leaping impulses and secret pleasures, that I had enjoyed in the disguise of Hyde. I made this choice perhaps with some unconscious reservation, for I neither gave up the house in Soho, nor destroyed the clothes of Edward Hyde, which still lay ready in my cabinet.
>
> —Robert Louis Stevenson, "The Strange Case of Dr. Jekyll and Mr. Hyde"

In this passage from Stevenson's famous story, Dr. Jekyll recalls a choice that he made but failed to live by—a resolution to never again transform himself into Edward Hyde. Jekyll remarks that he "made this choice perhaps with some unconscious reservation." What work does the word "unconscious" do in this sentence? When is a reservation—or an intention or a fear—rightly said to be unconscious? In this section, I'm going to draw on what's been said thus far in the present chapter in order to address these questions. I shall offer an account of what distinguishes a conscious mental state from an unconscious one.[5] I'll begin by elaborating on some of what was said about this topic when it was last explicitly discussed, in the dialogue that appeared in §1.3.

*   *   *

If asked what it is that distinguishes conscious mental states from unconscious ones, many philosophers and psychologists would, I think, answer along the following the lines: "Your mental state is conscious if

---

5. This does not mean that I'll be especially concerned with Freud or with psychoanalysis. We should bear in mind that Freud was not the first to acknowledge unconscious states of mind. ("The Strange Case of Dr. Jekyll and Mr. Hyde" was first published in 1886, almost a decade before the publication of Breuer and Freud's *Studies on Hysteria*.)

you know that you are in it. Your mental state is unconscious if you don't know that you're in it. To say that you, for example, unconsciously believe that no one could ever fall in love with you, is to say (1) that you believe that no one could ever fall in love with you and (2) that you don't know—you're unaware of the fact—that you believe this." Let's call this "the simple account of consciousness."[6]

A bit of reflection reveals that the simple account of consciousness is unsatisfactory. Imagine someone—call him Harry—who says: "My therapist tells me that I unconsciously believe no one could ever fall in love with me, and she's generally right about such things, so I suppose I must have this belief." Let's imagine that Harry's therapist *is* right about him and that Harry is justified in believing that she's right about him. Harry is, then, aware of his belief that no one could ever fall in love with him; he knows about it. According to the simple account, we should say that Harry's belief that no one could ever fall in love with him went from being unconscious to being conscious as a result of his conversation with his therapist. But we can imagine that Harry holds no such conscious belief. When asked about his future, Harry says, "Oh, I'm sure that eventually someone will fall in love with me, even though my therapist has convinced me that unconsciously I believe it's impossible that anyone should." This is a perfectly intelligible remark. What Harry's therapist has made him aware of is not that he is unlovable, but only that he unconsciously believes this to be so. The simple account, however, cannot allow for the intelligibility of what Harry wants to say about himself. According to the simple account, if someone is aware that he believes such-and-such, then his belief is conscious. But, in our example, Harry is aware of his unconscious belief that no one could fall in love with him.

The simple account of consciousness is *too* simple; it's not faithful to the way we use the words "conscious" and "unconscious." There is, however, a use of these words to which something like the simple account *is* faithful. The case of Harry demonstrates that there is a distinc-

6. Colin McGinn endorses the simple account when he writes: "This . . . raises the interesting problem of what makes a propositional attitude unconscious, of what differentiates conscious from unconscious reasons. . . . For a desire (say) to be unconscious is for its possessor not to know or believe that he has that desire" (McGinn 1979, 37).

tion to be drawn between two uses of the word "conscious" or "unconscious." First, there is a relatively unpuzzling use that is generally in place when the word "conscious" or "unconscious" is followed by the word "of" or "that." I might say, "Until the lights came on, I had been unconscious *of* the person in the seat next to me." Or: "Lois suddenly became conscious *that* she was the only patent attorney in the room." In such contexts, the word "conscious" means, roughly, *aware.* The corresponding use of "unconscious" means *unaware.* Among the things I might become aware, or conscious, *of* are my own states of mind. But to say that I am conscious of, e.g., my fear of abandonment is not to say either that I conscious*ly* fear abandonment or—what amounts to the same thing—that my fear of abandonment is conscious. Describing Harry as "conscious of unconsciously believing that no one could ever fall in love with him" (or "conscious of his unconscious belief that no one could ever fall in love with him") seems to involve a contradiction only if we confuse two senses of the word "conscious." It's one thing to be consciously angry or jealous or believing that such-and-such and quite another to be conscious of one's own anger, jealousy, or belief. We can think of this fact as providing us with a constraint on an adequate account of the distinction between conscious and unconscious mentality. Such an account should respect the difference between (a) someone's conscious*ly* believing or being conscious*ly* afraid, i.e., a belief or a fear's being conscious, rather than unconscious, and (b) someone's being conscious *of* her own belief or fear, i.e., conscious *that* she believes or fears such-and-such.

A variation on the simple account of consciousness might appear to provide us with what we need in order to meet this constraint. The view that I have in mind might be stated as follows: "The problem with the simple account is that it doesn't distinguish between *kinds* of knowledge. If my knowledge that I believe *p* is based upon only the testimony of my therapist, then—while I may be said to be conscious *of* my belief that *p*—I cannot be said to conscious*ly* believe *p*. The kind of self-knowledge that the word 'consciously' picks out is not knowledge by *testimony.* What it means for me to consciously believe that *p* (or to be consciously hopeful or afraid, etc.) is that I know my mental state via a *particular* cognitive mechanism—the mechanism by which I ordinarily find out about my own states of mind. It's tempting to refer to this mechanism as 'inner sense,' but perhaps we should just call it 'mechanism M.' What it means for one of my mental states to be conscious (i.e., for me to be conscious*ly* angry, sad, or whatever) is that I'm aware of it *via mechanism M.* What it means for one of my mental states to be unconscious is that—although I may be aware of it—I am not aware of it via mechanism M." Call this "the not-so-simple account of consciousness."

Much of §1.3's dialogue may be read as an extended criticism of the not-so-simple account of consciousness. I won't review that criticism here; for present purposes, a shorter argument will perhaps suffice. Let us stay with the case of Harry, who consciously believes that someone will eventually fall in love with him even though he is aware of his unconscious belief that no one could. The fact that, in this example, Harry's conscious and unconscious beliefs contradict each other helps to bring out the inadequacy of the simple account. But the need to distinguish between what someone is aware of believing and what he consciously believes does not depend on there being a flat-out contradiction between his conscious and unconscious beliefs. To see this, consider a variation on the example. Imagine that Harry says, "I unconsciously believe that no one could ever fall in love with me," whereupon he's asked whether anyone *could* fall in love with him. He answers, "Maybe; I'm not sure." Here too, Harry's belief that no one could fall in love with him is an unconscious one *of* which he is aware.

So, Harry's conscious opinions need not quite *contradict* his unconscious belief that no one could ever fall in love with him. Nevertheless, there *would* seem to be something wrong with Harry's saying, "I unconsciously believe that no one could ever fall in love with me; moreover, no one could ever fall in love with me." If Harry is willing to assert that no one could ever fall in love with him, then it's not right for him to say that he believes this unconsciously. We might think of this point in connection with Moore's paradox. Moore pointed out that it would be absurd for someone to utter a sentence of the form "I believe that p, and it is not the case that p." A number of writers have since noted that Moore's point does not hold for self-ascriptions of unconscious belief. In other words, there's nothing wrong with saying, "I *unconsciously* believe that p, and it is not the case that p." I'm calling something further to your attention—that, *prima facie*, there does seem to be something wrong with saying, "I unconsciously believe that p, and it *is* the case that p" (even though, as with Moore's paradox, both conjuncts might be true).[7] When we consider unconscious mental states, we find not only the failure of Moore's paradox but, as it were, the inversion of it. We might call this "Eroom's paradox."

Now, a bit of reflection on Eroom's paradox should, I think, leave us somewhat dissatisfied with the not-so-simple account of consciousness. The problem is this: However we envisage mechanism M, there would seem to be no absurdity in Harry's saying, "My belief that no one could ever love me is not known to me *via M;* moreover, no one could ever love me." Yet it *would* be absurd for Harry to say, "I unconsciously believe that no one could ever love me; moreover, no one could ever love me." Thus, given the not-so-simple account (according to which these utterances would be true under just the same conditions), Eroom's paradox looks very paradoxical indeed.

In §5.2, I considered an objection to the three-paragraph account of first-person authority, part of which went: "It seems implausible that the account can be getting things right about the kind of authority that it is meant to explain, given that it sheds no light on the other

---

7. This point should not be overstated. It *is* possible to imagine a situation in which a sentence of the form "I unconsciously believe that *p;* moreover, *p*" would be intelligible. Imagine that Harry's mother, who is a terrible driver, drives Harry to work every morning. Harry wishes that he were able to drive himself because he thinks it's dangerous to be a passenger in his mother's car. Indeed, he believes that his mother's inept driving is liable to result in his being injured or killed in a car accident. One day, Harry's psychoanalyst convinces him that he unconsciously believes that his mother means to murder him by poisoning his well water. In this situation, Harry could say, "I unconsciously believe that my mother is liable to harm me; moreover, my mother *is* liable to harm me. I believe both unconsciously and consciously that she's liable to harm me."

In the face of this example, it is natural to respond that, even so, Harry doesn't really believe the same thing about his mother both consciously and unconsciously. His conscious belief is that she's liable to harm him *by involving him in a car accident* while his unconscious belief is that she's liable to harm him *by deliberately poisoning his well water.* Where it makes sense for someone to utter a sentence of the form, "I unconsciously believe that *p;* moreover, *p*" (or "I believe that *p* both consciously *and* unconsciously"), we find that the contents of the conscious and unconscious beliefs in question can be further specified so as to display a difference between them. Notice that this is not true for sentences of the form "My friend believes that *p;* moreover, *p*" (or "My friend and I both believe that *p*"). My friend and I can be in, as it were, perfect agreement about *p.*

kinds." I mean to be raising the same kind of objection here concerning the not-so-simple account of consciousness: It is reasonable to expect that if we come to a satisfactory understanding of what distinguishes unconscious states of mind from conscious ones, we'll also understand what would be wrong with saying, e.g., "I unconsciously believe that my brother has ruined my bid for reelection; moreover, he has ruined it." But the not-so-simple account leaves Eroom's paradox looking completely mysterious. Thus, we have a reason for seeking another account of the distinction.

*   *   *

If the distinction between conscious and unconscious states of mind is neither a matter of what someone knows nor of how he knows it, what *is* it a matter of? Here let me remind you of another point that emerged in §1.3: we speak with first-person authority not about *all* our mental states, but only our conscious ones. I might learn in therapy that I harbor unconscious anger toward my sister, and having learned this, I might say to a friend, "I've discovered that I'm unconsciously angry with my sister." In such a circumstance, I would not speak with first-person authority. If my friend were to ask me why I take myself to harbor unconscious anger toward my sister, it wouldn't make sense for me to reply, "What do you mean? I'm just really angry with her." To repeat a conclusion that was reached in §1.3, the claims I make about my unconscious states of mind are only as good as the evidence that backs them up.

So: (1) when my anger (or intention or belief) is unconscious, I cannot ascribe it to myself with first-person authority. And: (2) as we saw earlier in the present chapter, when I *can* ascribe anger to myself with first-person authority, this is because I'm able to *express* it by so ascribing it. Taken together, these points suggest an alternative to the accounts of consciousness considered above. I want to claim that it is a defining characteristic of our unconscious mental states that we lack the ability to express them merely by self-ascribing them. Like all mental states, the unconscious ones may be expressed in our behavior. But what's distinctive about unconscious mental states is that we are unable to express them by self-ascribing them. If Harry unconsciously believes that he's unlovable, he might express this belief in any number of ways. But not by saying (or thinking),[8] "I believe that I'm unlovable." He *might* utter these words. He might say: "Well, you've convinced me. The only way to make sense of my behavior is by taking me to have this crazy unconscious belief. Unconsciously, I believe that I'm unlovable." Here, Harry expresses his opinion that he has a particular unconscious belief, but he does not express the unconscious belief; he doesn't express the belief that he is unlovable. (Indeed, he expresses the opposite opinion.)

The point may be put as follows: *Someone's mental state is conscious if he has an ability to express it merely by self-ascribing it.*[9] *If he lacks such an ability with respect to one of his mental states, it is unconscious.* On this account of

---

8. What if Harry were to think, "I believe that I'm unlovable" *unconsciously?* It's quite unclear what this means. What are we supposed be imagining here? It seems to me that I *can* imagine this: Harry's body is shared by two people, one of whom I call "Harry's conscious mind" and one of whom I call "Harry's unconscious mind." At some point, the latter thinks, "I believe that I'm unlovable." But this is to imagine *two* people (with misleading names), one of whom is thinking something. It's not to imagine one person, Harry, who is *unconsciously* thinking anything.

Some philosophers, e.g., Richard Rorty, treat unconscious mental states as if their existence indicated that each of us has more than one person residing in his body. I argue against this idea (criticizing Rorty 1991) in the paper from which most of the material in the present section is drawn, Finkelstein 1999a.

9. The word "merely" as I'm using it here is meant to forestall an objection that might be put as follows: "Imagine that you occasionally express your unconscious anger toward your sister by speaking in a peculiar, clipped tone of voice. One day, while speaking in this tone of voice, you say, 'My therapist tells me that I'm unconsciously angry with my sister, and I suppose she must be right.' Through your tone of voice, you express your anger toward your sister in a self-ascription of it, even though the anger is unconscious. What this case shows is that being able to express your state of mind by self-ascribing it is not a sufficient condition for the state's being conscious." When I say that someone's state of mind is conscious if he has an ability to express it *merely* by ascribing it to himself, I mean this: the sort of ability at issue is one that enables a person to express his state of mind in a self-ascription of it, where what matters—what carries the expressive force—isn't his tone of voice (or whether he is tapping his foot, or what he is wearing, or to whom he happens to be speaking), but simply the fact that he is giving voice to his sincere judgment about his own state of mind. That I might manage to express my unconscious anger in a self-ascription of it *via a clipped tone of voice* doesn't show that I have the relevant sort of expressive ability. When I am consciously angry, I can say in a neutral tone of voice, "I'm angry," and thereby express my anger.

the distinction between conscious and unconscious mental states, my intention to read Nick Hornby's most recent novel is conscious not by virtue of my knowing about it, or my knowing about it in a particular way, but by virtue of my being able to express it merely by saying, "I intend to read Nick Hornby's most recent novel."[10]

Note that this account helps us to see what's wrong with Eroom-paradoxical utterances. If Harry were to say, "No one could ever love me; moreover, I unconsciously believe that no one could ever love me," his utterance would be true just in case no one could ever love him *and* he lacked the ability to express his belief that no one could love him by self-ascribing it. What would be strange about such an utterance is that anyone who is in a position to assert sincerely that no one could ever love him should be able to express his belief that no one could love him by self-ascribing it.[11] Thus, given the account of consciousness that I have set out, we should expect Eroom-paradoxical utterances to be problematic.

*   *   *

Freud writes:

> From what I have so far said a neurosis would seem to be the result of a kind of ignorance—a not knowing about mental events that one ought to know of. . . . Now it would as a rule be very easy for a doctor experienced in analysis to guess what mental impulses had remained uncon-

10. I have discovered three other writers who point out that while it is possible for someone to ascribe an unconscious belief to himself, he does not thereby express the belief. These are Collins (1969), Rey (1988), and Moran (1997). While I'm sympathetic with a good deal of what these philosophers have to say, it seems to me that all of them understand the notion of expression too much in terms of a distinctive feature of *belief* self-ascription, viz., that when someone expresses his belief by saying, "I believe that p," he thereby commits himself to the truth of the claim that p. While this is a noteworthy feature of *one* kind of expression of *one* kind of mental state, if we understand the very notion of expression too much in terms of it, we lose our grip on what unconscious beliefs have in common with unconscious fears, wishes, and revulsion.

11. A person who is able to express his belief that p by saying "P" is, if he knows how the words "I believe that" function in English, *also* able to express his belief that p by saying, "I believe that p." The first ability, along with a knowledge of English, suffices for the second.

scious in a particular patient. So it ought not to be very difficult, either, for him to restore the patient by communicating his knowledge to him and so remedying his ignorance. . . .

If only that was how things happened! We came upon discoveries in this connection for which we were at first unprepared. Knowledge is not always the same as knowledge: there are different sorts of knowledge, which are far from equivalent psychologically. . . . If the doctor transfers his knowledge to the patient as a piece of information, it has no result. . . . The patient knows after this what he did not know before—the sense of his symptom; yet he knows it just as little as he did. Thus we learn that there is more than one kind of ignorance.   (Freud 1966, 280–281)

Freud expresses an important insight in this passage. It's one thing for me to know that I am, e.g., unconsciously angry with my sister and quite another thing for my anger toward her to become conscious. I have been trying, in effect, to explain how it is that "Knowledge is not always the same as knowledge." What Freud is calling to our attention in this passage turns out to be a distinction between someone's knowing that she is in a particular mental state and her having the ability to express her mental state merely by self-ascribing it.

Philosophers have, on the whole, tended to view the distinction between conscious and unconscious states of mind as an epistemic matter—a matter of whether, or how, a subject knows something. But to have an unconscious wish or fear is not essentially a matter of being ignorant of something. It is a matter of being unable to *do* something—of being unable to express one's state of mind in a particular way.[12]

5.5. Between Conscious and Unconscious

Tevya: Do you love me?
Golda: I'm your wife!
Tevya: I know! But do you love me?

12. I have, in this section, been speaking about unconscious mental states: unconscious intentions, fears, and the like. I have not spoken of anything that could be called *the* unconscious. In Finkelstein 1999a, I explain how a story along these lines might accommodate the unconscious, and I say more about how unconscious states of mind may be related to conscious ones.

Golda: Do I love him? For twenty-five years I've cooked for him, cleaned
  for him, starved with him. Twenty-five years my bed is his. If that's not
  love what is?

Tevya: Then you love me?

Golda: I suppose I do.

Tevya: And I suppose I love you too.

Both: It doesn't change a thing, but even so, after twenty-five years, it's
  nice to know!
　　　　　　　　　　　　—"Do You Love Me?" by Sheldon Harnick and Jerry Bock

Helen has a new boyfriend. After she's been involved with him for a
couple of months, a friend asks her if she *loves* him. She replies: "Well,
I feel comfortable when I'm with him, and I'm really attracted to him.
On the other hand, I don't always like his politics, and he talks too
much about his therapy sessions. Still, he's considerate, not just with
me but with everybody—with waiters and salespeople. I admire that.
And I like the way he looks and smells. Oh, and you know how, usually,
I can't stand being around people when they're sick? When Harry had
the flu, I stopped in almost every evening after work to bring him food
and check up on him. So, yes, I suppose I love him."

Think of an honest avowal of "I want you to stop humming that irritating song" as located at one end of a continuum. At the other end lie
statements such as "I've come to the conclusion that I'm unconsciously
jealous of my sister's success." The first self-ascription is an expression
of the desire that it's a self-ascription of. The second self-ascription is
not an expression of the jealousy that it's a self-ascription of. It's an expression of the speaker's *opinion* that she is jealous, but not an expression of jealousy. The first self-ascription is not based on evidence about
the speaker's behavior. The second self-ascription is.

When Helen says, "So, yes, I suppose I love him"—when she avows,
in this way, her love for Harry—is this an expression of love or merely
an expression of her opinion concerning her own emotional state? Is
what she says based on evidence? Which of the two self-ascriptions just
considered is Helen's avowal like? As I imagine Helen, her avowal is a
little bit like each of those self-ascriptions; it lies somewhere in the
middle of the continuum. It is, to a certain extent, an expression of
love, but only to a certain extent. It is, to a certain extent, based on evidence, but, again, only to a certain extent.

In the last section, §5.4, I argued that whether a mental state is conscious or unconscious depends on whether a subject has the ability to express it merely by self-ascribing it. Does Helen have the ability to express her love for Harry merely by self-ascribing it? The answer would seem to be: Sort of. She has an inchoate ability. In time, if her relationship with Harry continues to go well, then it ought to be fully realized. (She should also come to love him more, but this is not the same point.) Thus, if what I said in §5.4 is correct, we should expect that there won't be any clear answer to the question of whether Helen's love for Harry is, at the time of the above-described conversation, conscious or unconscious. And, it seems to me, this is what we find if we ask ourselves how it would be most natural to describe Helen's state. I find myself wanting to say that her love is a little bit conscious or that while it's not quite conscious, it's not really unconscious either.

In §§5.1–5.3, I claimed that the authority we accord to mental state avowals should be understood as a matter of their expressing the very states that they are avowals of. If this is right, then we might expect Helen—whose answer to her friend's question only sort-of-expresses her love—to speak with partial, or a little bit of, first-person authority. Both in Chapter 1 and in the beginning of the present chapter, I characterized the phenomenon of first-person authority in terms of these two facts: (1) If you want to know my psychological condition, I'm usually the best person to ask and (2) there's no need for me to consider behavioral evidence in order for me to say what I'm thinking or feeling. When Helen addresses the question of whether or not she loves Harry, does she speak with first-person authority? Well, she *does* need to consider the evidence.[13] But her relation to this evidence is not what it would be if she were speaking about someone else's state of mind or about one of her own unconscious psychological states. I said in §5.4 that a person's statements about her own unconscious mental states are only as good as the evidence she has to back them up. This isn't

---

13. Notice that only *some* of this evidence is behavioral. When Helen says, "I like the way he looks and smells," she's adducing evidence, but it's not behavioral evidence. Insofar as she is inferring that she loves Harry (and to a certain extent, this *is* what she's doing, but only to a certain extent), this inference is based on a number of premises that are, for her, not themselves epistemically justified. I'll have more to say about this kind of inference in §6.4.

true of Helen's statement about loving Harry. To a certain extent, it transcends the evidential considerations that lead up to it.[14] We might say that her avowal *leans,* rather than rests squarely, on the evidence. Thus, I *do* find myself wanting to say that Helen speaks with partial, or a little bit of, first-person authority. If her relationship with Harry flourishes, then perhaps in time she'll speak with more of this kind of authority when she avows her love for him.

To the extent that a self-ascription of love, anger, or even pain leans on evidence, both consciousness and first-person authority go missing. Or, to put the point differently, to the extent that consciousness and first-person authority go missing, there is (to this extent) a genuine epistemic question for the subject about whether she loves or is angry or is in pain. Here, consider the last line of my epigraph for this section—the last line of the song "Do You Love Me?" from *Fiddler on the Roof.* Golda and Tevya sing together, "It doesn't change a thing, but even so, after twenty-five years, it's nice to know!" *What's* nice to know? Well, it's nice for Tevya to know that Golda loves him, and it's nice for Golda to know that he loves her. But I would suggest that we can hear more than this in that line: it's *also* nice for Golda to know that *she* loves Tevya and for Tevya to know that *he* loves her. To the extent that Golda's avowal of love leans on evidence, it represents an epistemic achievement; she's come to *know* something about herself.[15]

In Chapter 1, when I was introducing new detectivism, I quoted the following from Russell's *Analysis of Mind:*

> I believe that the discovery of our own motives can only be made by the
> same process by which we discover other people's, namely, the process
> of observing our actions and inferring the desire which could prompt

14. But it doesn't *completely* transcend them. We *can* imagine a scenario in which Helen's love suddenly becomes fully conscious after she has spent a little time talking or thinking through Harry's good qualities and her own feelings about them. But as I'm imagining Helen's conversation with her friend, this isn't what happens; she's hasn't quite kicked away the evidential ladder when she reaches her conclusion (hence, the word "suppose" in "So, yes, I suppose I love him").

15. Do I mean to deny that the person who says, "I want you to stop humming that irritating song," *knows* that she wants the humming to stop? No; I don't mean to deny this. But if we do choose to speak of knowledge in such a case, it's knowledge of a rather special sort. See §6.4.

them. A desire is "conscious" when we have told ourselves that we have it.   (Russell 1921, 31)

Russell isn't crazy; we *do*—some of us more than others—try to discover our own states of mind by making inferences on the basis of behavioral evidence.[16] But he gets something very wrong in 1921: to the extent that someone tells herself *on the basis of evidence* that she desires a particular thing (or that she loves someone), her desire (or her love) is, to that extent, precisely *not* "conscious."

5.6. The Logical Space of Animate Life

Recall poor Franny, who, upon groaning her distaste for the weak coffee that she's been served, is asked what her groan was an expression of. When she answers, "I groaned because of how much I detest this coffee," she speaks with a kind of first-person authority about her groan, even though she isn't—or, rather, it doesn't make sense to describe her as—"expressing a groan." In the course of trying to account for this kind of authority, I suggested (in §5.3) that we understand the relation between a mental state and its expression as a species of a broader genus, a genus that includes the sort of relation that Franny's remark bears to her groan. Although my focus was first-person authority, what was beginning to emerge in that discussion (as well as in the discussion of the CEO and of Wittgenstein's appropriation of the context principle) has somewhat broader implications. What was emerging is a picture in which some things—e.g., an expectation, the circumstances that occasion it, and its expression in act, word, or thought —must, in order to come into full view, be understood together, in light of one another. Such things have, we might say, a particular kind of intelligibility. We might speak here of a distinctive logical space in which we locate mental items and their expressions along with the circumstances against whose background they have the significances that they do. I'm tempted to call this "the logical space of persons," for to see a thing as a person requires that we make it intelligible in this way—that we understand some of its states as hanging together with its circumstances and its movements in a way that the states, circum-

16. And, again, not only *behavioral* evidence.

stances, and movements of, e.g., clouds do not hang together. But for reasons that will emerge in the next chapter, I'll call it instead "the logical space of animate life."

By speaking in terms of a distinctive logical space, I am echoing a note that was sounded well before we met Franny. In Chapter 3, I noted that McDowell understands pains and other occurrent mental items as figuring, along with believings and knowings, in what he, following Sellars, calls "the logical space of reasons." According to McDowell, pains figure in the space of reasons in the following sense at least: My pain constitutes my epistemic justification for ascribing pain to myself; when I say that I'm in pain, I do so *on the basis of* the pain. As we'll see, McDowell not only defends this idea; he takes Wittgenstein to defend it as well. He suggests, moreover, that "Wittgenstein's philosophy of mind can be encapsulated in the remark that mental life is lived in the space of reasons" (1998d, 296). One of my aims in Chapter 6 will be to show what is wrong with this suggestion in part by bringing out why it would be less misleading to say that, according to Wittgenstein, mental life is lived in the logical space of animate life.

Sensations, Animals, and Knowledge

In the concluding section of his essay "One Strand in the Private Language Argument," John McDowell observes that "[i]t is common nowadays for philosophers of mind to invoke a distinction between sapience and sentience, in such a way as to suggest that there are two simply different problem areas within their branch of philosophy" (McDowell 1998d, 295). This way of mapping out the terrain in the philosophy of mind would locate discussions of intentionality at a distance from talk about sensations, "qualia," or "raw feels." McDowell points out that Wittgenstein's writing does not fit well into a landscape that is divided in this way:

> He is plainly interested in what other philosophers call "propositional attitudes" (e.g., in the remarks about expectation, etc., in the §400's), and equally plainly interested in the difficulties that philosophers get into over "raw feels" (e.g., in §290), and the latter interest does not look like an interest in a "residual problem," or even like an interest that we ought to regard as significantly removed from the former. . . . (1998d, 296)

According to McDowell, a lesson we might learn from Wittgenstein is that "there is something wrong with the supposed distinction" (1998d, 296), i.e., that making sense of sentience ought not to appear a completely separate task from understanding sapience.

McDowell is onto something important here: Wittgenstein does see connections between sapience and sentience that tend to go unnoticed in contemporary philosophy of mind. I'll argue, however, that he (McDowell) misdescribes this strand in Wittgenstein's thought. He attributes to Wittgenstein what, in Chapter 3, I referred to as "the middle path account of inner awareness," according to which items in a stream of consciousness, e.g., pains, are constituted by the actualization of conceptual capacities. This does bring sentience and sapience into contact. But if what I said in Chapter 3 is right, it fails to do justice to the richness of experiential life. And if what I'll say in the present chapter is right, it likewise fails to do justice to Wittgenstein's thought. One of my aims here is to provide a better account than McDowell does of what he gets right when he remarks that, for Wittgenstein, sapience and sentience "are not two simply different problem areas" (1998d, 296). In what follows, I shall be asking not only how sentience is related to sapience, but also how our minds are like, and unlike, the minds of nonlinguistic animals. I'll end with a few remarks on the question of whether, given what I've said in this book, we can rightly be said to *know* our own conscious inner states.

6.1. "But Isn't the Beginning the Sensation—Which I Describe?"

As we saw in Chapter 3, McDowell's views about both outer and inner sense are motivated in significant part by the thought that we must not allow ourselves to be seduced by the Myth of the Given. He believes that Wittgenstein too is moved by what amounts to this thought in (what commentators call) the Private Language Argument. According to McDowell, the real mistake made by the interlocutor sometimes referred to as "the private linguist" is to embrace the idea of the Given in connection with judgments concerning our own sensations—the idea that what justifies, e.g., my judgment that I have a headache is an inner item that, in itself, does not involve the operations of conceptual capacities. McDowell urges us to read Wittgenstein as struggling, sometimes not entirely successfully, to articulate a view along the following lines: My pain is through-and-through conceptual; it includes no preconceptual component. When I judge that I am in pain, I don't first experience an unconceptualized item and only then classify it as a pain; my pain is not like that of a dog or an infant with a conceptual or classificatory component *added* to it. Rather, my pain just *is* a conceptual awareness.

One argument against this sort of position might be put as follows: "If we grant that there is no part of a subject's sensation that is independent of her classifying it as this or that, then the pain itself seems to disappear. We're left imagining a bogus 'classification' where there is really nothing to be classified." This is tricky ground, and McDowell suggests that Wittgenstein does not always negotiate it as well as he might. He writes, "If we read Wittgenstein in this framework, we might want to question his sureness of foot in passages like this," whereupon he quotes the following from §304 of the *Investigations:*

> "And yet you again and again reach the conclusion that the sensation itself is a *nothing.*"—Not at all. It is not a *something,* but not a *nothing* either! The conclusion was only that a nothing would serve just as well as a something about which nothing could be said. We have only rejected the grammar which tries to force itself on us here.

What could Wittgenstein mean when he says, "It is not a *something,* but not a *nothing* either"? As McDowell reads *PI* §304, the point could be put thus: A sensation, e.g., the pain in my wrist, is "not a *nothing*": it is real, not mere illusion or fancy. Nonetheless, it's not anything over and above my conceptual awareness of it, and this is why Wittgenstein allows that it is "not a *something*"—because he holds that it is not as *robust* a something as is, say, a pebble or a wristwatch. According to McDowell, we should question Wittgenstein's "sureness of foot" here, not because this is the wrong account of sensations, but because of the misleading way in which the account is stated. To allow that the sensation is "not a *something*" is to encourage the interlocutor's worry that, on Wittgenstein's view of inner awareness, the sensation disappears.

As McDowell reads Wittgenstein on sensations and self-awareness, *PI* §304 does not present his "best moves in this area" (1998d, 285); another section that comes a bit earlier in the *Investigations* does. This section, §290, figures as McDowell's primary datum in support of the idea that Wittgenstein would have us embrace the middle path account of inner awareness. It reads as follows:

> What I do is not, of course, to identify my sensation by criteria: but to repeat an expression. But this is not the *end* of the language-game: it is the beginning.
>
> But isn't the beginning the sensation—which I describe?—Perhaps this word "describe" tricks us here. I say "I describe my state of mind"

and "I describe my room." You need to call to mind the differences between the language-games.   (*PI* §290)

According to McDowell, this section of the *Investigations* expresses more clearly than does §304 the view that while a sensation *is* a something, it is a *kind* of something that is not present prior to or independently of its being brought under a concept:

> At *PI* §290 Wittgenstein's interlocutor says "But isn't the beginning the sensation—which I describe?" This expresses, surely for the purposes of criticizing it . . . the idea that the "item recognized" (the sensation) is present anyway, independently of being brought under a concept ("described")—that is something which happens later. . . . The notion of a limiting case of a particular/general or subject/predicate structure . . . is a way of keeping "describe" without implying the idea that Wittgenstein is clearly trying to avoid: that what describing here amounts to is bringing under a concept an item that is there in consciousness anyway, whether or not any conceptual structure is in place.   (1998d, 284–285)

As McDowell reads §290, it shows us how to understand §304. Both sections express Wittgenstein's commitment to the middle path account of inner awareness—to the idea that a sensation is nothing over and above a subject's conceptual awareness of it.

*   *   *

In §290, when Wittgenstein's interlocutor asks, "But isn't the beginning the sensation—which I describe?" he is inquiring about the relation between his sensation and what he *says* about it. Notice, however, that in the above quotation from McDowell, *PI* §290 is recast so that its topic is not the relation between a sensation and a spoken remark but, instead, that between a sensation and its "being brought under a concept." As McDowell notes, his reading depends on "transpos[ing] the thought that is expressed here [in §290] with reference to language into a parallel thought about the employment of concepts" (1998d, 285). The transposed thought, the thought about concepts, could be put like this: a sensation is not first felt and only then brought under a concept; rather, it is conceptualized from the start.

This, McDowell thinks, is a "parallel thought" to the one actually expressed in §290 concerning what we *say* about our sensations.

But is it really? Let us ask: What would be the, as it were, *untransposed* version of the thought about concepts that McDowell articulates on Wittgenstein's behalf? In other words, given McDowell's reading of what a transposed version of §290 says about the employment of concepts, what must the section, as it actually appears in the *Investigations,* be saying about language use? If the transposed version of §290 says that I cannot have a sensation prior to putting it under a concept, then the untransposed, original version should say that I cannot have a sensation prior to describing it in words, i.e., that I cannot first have a sensation and only later remark on it. But this thesis is unsatisfactory to the point of being absurd. It cannot be what Wittgenstein means to be defending in §290.

So: McDowell says that *PI* §290 represents Wittgenstein's "best moves" in the area of sensations and self-awareness. Yet, as he seems committed to reading it, this section arrives at an absurd conclusion unless it is recast in such a way as to change its subject matter. We should, therefore, view his account of §290 with considerable suspicion. Moreover, since he understands §304 ("It is not a *something . . .*") in light of §290, we should question his reading of this section of the *Investigations* as well.

*   *   *

If we reject McDowell's interpretation of *PI* §290, how might we understand Wittgenstein when he says, regarding the avowal of a sensation, "But this is not the *end* of the language-game: it is the beginning"? Let's follow the advice offered at the end of §290 and "call to mind the differences" between describing a room and describing one's own state of mind. Imagine that, upon entering the kitchen of a house whose purchase you are considering, you say: "This room is a problem. The cabinets look cheap, and there's less counter space than I'm used to. It does get a lot of light, though." Such a description might be characterized as the last move in a little language-game. Before you can describe the room, you need to look it over. Only after you have looked around—observed things—are you entitled to talk about what you have seen. So the moves in this language-game are (1) observe and (2) describe (or, if you prefer, (1) observe, (2) judge, and (3) describe). The describing comes at the *end* of the game—after the observing. Wittgenstein's point in §290 is that we need to distinguish *this* sort of language-game from the sort in which you're engaged when you describe one of your own sensations. You are entitled to say, "I have a sharp pain in my wrist," without needing to do any observing (or judging) first. In the language-game of describing your own sensation, the first thing that you do—the first move you make—is the describing. Thus, when you say that you are in pain, "this is not the *end* of the language-game: it is the beginning."

If we read *PI* §290 this way, then we can indeed "transpose the thought that is expressed here with reference to language into a parallel thought about the employment of concepts." A parallel thought about the employment of concepts could be put as follows: Even if I don't *say* that I'm feeling a pain, I am able to apply the concept *pain* to my sensation *without first inwardly observing anything.* If I get a headache while lecturing, I may *think* to myself, "I'm getting a headache," and I can do this without needing to observe my own behavior.[1] Now, I don't doubt that Wittgenstein would accept this thought about the employment of concepts along with the thought expressed in §290. But to accept this is not to commit oneself to the middle path account of inner awareness.

*　　*　　*

According to the middle path account of inner awareness, when I say that I am in pain, my statement is justified *by* my pain, which is constituted by conceptual capacities in operation. If Wittgenstein does not, in fact, commit himself to any such claim, what *does* he think justifies an avowal of pain? If we examine the material immediately preceding §290 in the *Investigations,* we find that the following answer emerges: *Nothing.* According to Wittgenstein, self-ascriptions of pain are not epistemically grounded; nothing justifies them. So, at §289, he writes:

> "When I say 'I am in pain' I am at any rate justified *before myself.*"—What does that mean? Does it mean: "If someone else could know what I am calling 'pain,' he would admit that I was using the word correctly"?
>
> To use a word without justification does not mean to use it without right.

1. See §§5.2–5.3 for a discussion of this sort of self-ascription.

Ordinarily, an expression of pain—a pained wince, for example—requires no epistemic justification, and according to Wittgenstein, avowals of pain *are* such expressions.[2] A question like "What are your grounds for saying that you have a sharp pain in your wrist?" presupposes what, in §288, Wittgenstein calls "the abrogation of the normal language-game with the expression of a sensation." It is not on the basis of epistemic grounds that I express my pain, either when I wince or when I say, "I have a sharp pain in my wrist."

McDowell does not fail to notice that *PI* §289 appears to speak against his reading of §290. He tries to defuse this appearance by claiming that when, in §289, Wittgenstein talks of using a word "without justification," he means to be rejecting only a particular *kind* of justification—justification that appeals to the Given (1998d, 286). Here, as in §304, Wittgenstein appears, on McDowell's account of him, to be putting his point in a misleading way. I want to suggest that in his reading of this part of the *Investigations,* McDowell is in the grip of a false dilemma. In order to help bring this into view, let me call your attention to the following quotation (part of which we looked at in §3.1) from *Mind and World:* "[I]t is one thing to be exempt from blame, on the ground that the position we find ourselves in can be traced ultimately to brute force; it is quite another thing to have a justification. In effect, the idea of the Given offers exculpations where we wanted justifications" (1996, 8). In a footnote, McDowell explains why he chooses to use the word "exculpations" rather than "excuses":

> What I want is an analogue to the sense in which if someone is found in a place from which she has been banished, she is exculpated by the fact that she was deposited there by a tornado. Her arriving there is completely removed from the domain of what she is responsible for; it is not that she is still responsible, but there is a basis for mitigating any sanctions.   (1996, 8)

Think of these passages as issuing a warning: If a person were merely caused to make some "judgment" by being exposed to a bit of the Given, she would be no more responsible for it than she would be for her location if she were carried off by a tornado. We must take care that our preferred account of perceptual awareness can accommodate this fact—that it allows for perceptual judgments that are justified, not

2. Or, anyway, they are akin to them in this respect (see §4.3).

merely exculpated. Let us grant this point. For present purposes, the crucial move is the one that comes next. Turning his attention from perceptual judgments to what he calls "judgements of 'inner sense,'" McDowell proceeds as if the same sort of warning would be apposite. We must, he thinks, take care that our preferred account of inner experience allows us to represent a subject's judgments about her own sensations and thoughts as justified, not merely exculpated. He assumes, in effect, that we must choose between saying (1) that a self-ascription of pain is the result of what we might call brute causation—something to be understood in the way that we'd understand the location of a person who had been deposited somewhere by a tornado and (2) that such self-ascriptions typically express epistemically justified judgments (where nothing can count as epistemically justifying a judgment unless it has propositional content, i.e., unless it "contains a claim").[3]

Wittgenstein would reject this dilemma, and we should too. One moral that could be drawn from what I have been saying since Chapter 4 is that the relation between a pain and a subject's ascription of it to herself is, typically, neither a matter of epistemic justification nor, as it were, mere causation.[4] When someone complains of a splitting headache, she does not judge on this or that basis that she is in pain.[5] Rather, she expresses her pain. And while I don't mean to deny that a pain may be understood to cause its expression, the relation between pain and expression is not *merely* causal. A pain and its expression make sense together in something like the way that two parts of a single sentence do. To revert to language that I introduced at the end of the last chapter, a pain and its expression hang together in the logical space of animate life.

3. As we saw in Chapter 3, according to McDowell, a genuine epistemic justifier must be, for the subject, *to the effect that* such-and-such. (On the middle path account of inner awareness, what justifies a self-ascription of pain is an impression to the effect that the subject is in pain.)

4. At least not if one accepts a conception of epistemic justification much like McDowell's (or Davidson's or Sellars's or Wittgenstein's). For more on this point, see n. 14 in §6.4.

5. She does not *judge* at all. I believe that McDowell would, today, agree that one needn't make a judgment in order to honestly avow a headache. (See n. 7 in §3.2.) But, if I am reading him correctly, he would retain the idea that when someone issues such an avowal, she is, typically, expressing an epistemically justified belief, and this too should be rejected.

McDowell is drawn to the middle path account of inner awareness by a desire to steer clear of the Myth of the Given *while* accommodating the idea that whenever one describes one's own state of mind— even if only by saying, "My head hurts"—one is epistemically justified, not merely exculpated, in so doing. He attributes the middle path account to Wittgenstein, appealing for support to a section of the *Investigations* in which Wittgenstein says: "You need to call to mind the differences between the language-games," i.e., between a language-game in which one describes one's own state of mind and one in which one describes a room. But, for Wittgenstein, part of what it means to take these differences seriously is that one does not go on trying to accommodate the idea that whenever one describes one's own state of mind, one is epistemically justified.

6.2. "It Is Not a *Something,* but Not a *Nothing* Either!"

Let's return to *PI*§304, the section that includes the following exchange:

> "And yet you again and again reach the conclusion that the sensation itself is a *nothing*."—Not at all. It is not a *something*, but not a *nothing* either!

As I noted earlier, McDowell hears "It is not a *something*, but not a *nothing* either!" as an expression of Wittgenstein's commitment to the middle path account of inner awareness. He writes:

> Wittgenstein's willingness to say that the sensation is "not a something" is a response to a thought that one might put . . . like this: in the kind of case in question we have at best . . . a limiting case of the idea of an object that we can designate and classify. The idea of encountering a particular is in place here *only because* the experience involves a concept (*pain,* say, or *toothache*): the particular has no status except as what is experienced as instantiating the concept.   (1998d, 284)

According to McDowell, while this is the correct view of sensations, Wittgenstein puts things misleadingly when he allows that a sensation is "not a *something*." For this lends credibility to his interlocutor's suspicion that, given what Wittgenstein has said prior to §304, the inner item of which one is supposedly aware turns out not really to exist:

[S]ometimes that item does seem to disappear, as when it is said not to be a something. (1998d, 285)

Wittgenstein could, and perhaps should, have said something more like this. The sensation (the pain, say) is a perfectly good something— an object if you like of concept-involving awareness. (1998d, 283)

As we have seen, McDowell thinks that Wittgenstein is not at his best in §304; the moves he makes are not as "subtle" (1998d, 285) as elsewhere in his writing on the topic of sensations. I'm going to suggest a rather different reading of *PI* §304—one that allows us to see this section as (1) supplementing what was said in §290 about the need to attend to the expressive dimension of sensation avowals and (2) lacking nothing in subtlety.

PI §304 comprises two paragraphs. The first reads as follows:

"But you will surely admit that there is a difference between pain-behaviour accompanied by pain and pain-behaviour without any pain?"—Admit it? What greater difference could there be?—"And yet you again and again reach the conclusion that the sensation itself is a *nothing*."—Not at all. It is not a *something*, but not a *nothing* either! The conclusion was only that a nothing would serve just as well as a something about which nothing could be said. We have only rejected the grammar which tries to force itself on us here.

What does Wittgenstein mean when he says, "We have only rejected the grammar which tries to force itself on us here"? What sort of grammar tries to force itself on us when we think about sensations, and what is gained by rejecting this grammar?

Here, we may be guided by the section that immediately follows *PI* §304:

"But you surely cannot deny that, for example, in remembering, an inner process takes place."—What gives the impression that we want to deny anything? When one says "Still, an inner process does take place here"—one wants to go on: "After all, you *see* it." (*PI* §305)

Notice that the topic has shifted: whereas Wittgenstein and his interlocutor were discussing *pain* in §304, here in §305 they are talking about *remembering*. This sort of shift is characteristic of Wittgenstein's writing. As he understands things, many of the problems that confront us when we think philosophically about sensations arise as well when we consider intentional mental phenomena. I'll return to this point later on. For the present, I want to focus on how §305 can help us to understand "the grammar which tries to force itself on us" in §304. §305 suggests that this is the grammar that would incline us to say, "After all, you *see* it." What's at issue is an impulse to represent us as knowing what goes on in our own minds by a kind of inner observation—as if our mental states and processes were like physical ones, at least insofar as we ourselves can *see* them, even if no one else can. We could say that the grammar which tries to force itself on us is that of observable physical states, processes, and objects.

Now, how should we understand the moment in §304 that McDowell suggests is misleading and unsubtle, the moment at which Wittgenstein presents his interlocutor with a paradox: "It is not a *something*, but not a *nothing* either"? We can begin to address this question by considering §304's second paragraph:

> The paradox disappears only if we make a radical break with the idea that language always functions in one way, always serves the same purpose: to convey thoughts—which may be about houses, pains, good and evil, or anything you please.

Think of the phrase "to convey thoughts" as here playing the same role as the word "describe" did in §290. Wittgenstein's point is not to deny that when someone speaks about her own pain, she conveys a thought; it is, rather, to force us "to call to mind the differences between the language-games" in which we are said to "convey thoughts." I might convey a thought by saying either (1) "The paint on the side of the house is starting to peel" or (2) "My wrist is starting to hurt." But the language-games are different. When I say (1), I report something that I've observed (or learned about in some other way). I don't do this when I say (2); instead I express a sensation. To "make a radical break with the idea that language always functions in one way" is to bring *this* distinction into focus. It is to stop philosophizing as if our talk about pains functioned in more or less the same way as our talk about houses.

How does giving up the idea that language functions in just one way make the paradox disappear? Well, there *are* contexts in which it would make sense to employ the phrase "the sensation itself." But when the interlocutor of *PI* §304 complains, "And yet you again and again reach the conclusion that the sensation itself is a *nothing*," we should hear this, Wittgenstein thinks, as mixing up language-games in such a way as to say nothing at all.[6] A couple of paragraphs back, I said that when, in §304, Wittgenstein speaks of "the grammar which tries to force itself on us," this may be understood as referring to the grammar of observable physical states, processes, and objects. We might dwell on the word "tries" as it figures in this phrase: the grammar to which Wittgenstein refers doesn't *quite* force itself upon us; it merely tries to. If the interlocutor really *were* using words like "pain" and "sensation" with the grammar of observable physical items, then he wouldn't be moved to say in §303, "I can only *believe* that someone else is in pain, but I *know* it if I am." But he is using these terms without *any* settled grammar; he is, as it were, shifting back and forth between the grammar of sensation-talk and the grammar of talk about physical things in such a way as to say nothing.[7]

Now, it's important to Wittgenstein that to reply to this sort of gram-

6. In §4.1, I said, "As long as we try to 'undress' words—to strip away the context and understand them as squiggles—we will be unable to make sense of the suggestion that 'there is a way of grasping a rule which is *not* an *interpretation*.'" If we imagine that the grammar of sensations resembles that of observable physical items more than it in fact does, we'll be inclined to try the same sort of undressing here—to insist that sensations be considered in isolation from the expressive linkages that are characteristic of the logical space of animate life. This, I suggest, is how we should hear the interlocutor's "sensation itself." In §4.1, I argued that Wittgenstein is not interested in offering an account of how it is that meaningful words, considered apart from the contexts in which they can be intelligible as more than dead noises or squiggles, manage to *be* meaningful words. Similarly, Wittgenstein's response to his interlocutor's complaint in §304 is not to offer an account of "the sensation itself."

It should give us pause when McDowell speaks of "Wittgenstein's willingness to say that the sensation is 'not a something'" (1998d, 284). Wittgenstein doesn't, in fact, exhibit a willingness to say that "the sensation" is not a something. He says this about "the sensation itself," where the interlocutor's use of these words signals his desire to make sense of pain apart from what Wittgenstein thinks of as the sort of context in which it is intelligible that a creature should feel pain.

7. If Wittgenstein's interlocutor allowed the grammar of observable physical items to *fully* shape his thinking about sensations, then he would sound more like a new detectivist than he does. Instead of saying, "I can only *believe* that someone else is in pain, but I *know* it if I am," he'd say that we know our own sensations thanks to the same sorts of fallible cognitive processes that allow us to know the sensations of others. But Wittgenstein's interlocutor isn't drawn to new detectivism. My sense is that

matical conflation with *either* agreement or denial would be to participate in it. To do so would be to grant that one's interlocutor had managed, at least, to posit something ("the sensation itself"), even if the
thing posited turned out not to exist. But a bit of nonsense does not
posit anything. Thus, when Wittgenstein says, "It is not a *something*, but
not a *nothing* either!" he is rejecting "the grammar which tries to force
itself on us"—the, as it were, attempted incursion of one grammar into
another—while signaling that he is rejecting *only* this, not the existence of some (successfully) posited inner item. So understood, Wittgenstein's odd reply to his interlocutor no longer sounds quite so paradoxical. "The paradox disappears" if we make the radical break that
he calls for.

Cora Diamond notes that "[p]assages like §304 need to be *heard* in
the mind's ear; one has to hear what they are directed against" (Diamond 1991, 264). When Wittgenstein says, "It is not a *something*, but
not a *nothing* either!" he is speaking *to* an interlocutor who has just accused him of denying the existence of "the sensation itself." Rather
than offering what we might think of as a straightforward answer to
this charge ("You're misunderstanding me; I acknowledge the existence of the sensation itself" or "You're right, I deny its existence"), he
replies with what sounds like a paradox. This reply is meant to *stop*
us—to force us to think about the interlocutor's use of the words
"the sensation itself" and, thereby, help us see that, as these words are
being used *here,* they say nothing. *Pace* McDowell, Wittgenstein's odd-
sounding reply to "And yet you again and again reach the conclusion that the sensation itself is a *nothing*" would not have been better
worded if he had said instead, "Actually, it's a limiting case of a something."

One point that emerges from this discussion is that the "paradox" of
§304 is not the statement of any thesis about what sensations are. That
McDowell allows himself to think otherwise, that he hears it as an artic-
ulation of the claim that a sensation is nothing over and above a sub-

Wittgenstein himself doesn't find new detectivism appealing enough to spend much
time engaging with it. Instead, he tries to show that if one presses on *old* detectivism,
it dissolves into nonsense—hence, §304's "a something about which nothing can be
said," a phrase that (after §261) we should recognize as nonsense. (If *nothing* can be
said about it, then it can't be said even to be a something.)

ject's conceptual awareness of it, bespeaks an uncharacteristic failure on his part to bear in mind the kind of philosopher that Wittgenstein is—one who doesn't want to be advancing theses of this sort.[8] We should not expect Wittgenstein to express views that could be put: "Sensations [or emotions or attitudes] are nothing more than. . . ." He's not *that* kind of a philosopher. He is the kind who says:

> We ask "What does 'I am frightened' really mean, what am I referring to when I say it?" And of course we find no answer, or one that is inadequate.
>
> The question is: "In what sort of context does it occur?" (*PI* II§ix; see also *Z* §§532–533, quoted below.)

*   *   *

I have been focusing on *PI* §§290 and 304 in part because McDowell adduces them as his main textual support for attributing the middle path account of inner awareness to Wittgenstein. I've argued that this attribution is not merely unsupported by §§290 and 304; it cannot be reconciled with them. You may recall from Chapter 3 that, in *Mind and World*, McDowell urges us to "think about 'inner sense' in parallel with 'outer sense' to the fullest extent that is possible" (1996, 22). This recommmendation is consistent with Wittgenstein's position as McDowell understands it. But, if what I've been saying since Chapter 4 is on the right track, Wittgenstein would, in fact, resist any such recommendation. Indeed, *PI* §§290 and 304 should, I think, be read *as* resisting any such recommendation. We need, Wittgenstein says in §304, to "make a radical break with the idea that language functions in one way." We make this break when we notice how very *different* the grammar of sensation avowals is from that of perceptual reports—when we stop trying to think about "inner sense" in parallel with seeing and hearing and instead attend to the expressive dimension of sensation avowals.

8. By way of contrast, consider the following objection that McDowell adduces against Wright: "[A]voiding platonism is supposed to require of us, according to Wittgenstein as Wright reads him, substantive and—one might naturally think—distinctly unprepossessing theses of a discernibly philosophical kind, certainly not theses that 'it would never be possible to debate . . . because everyone would agree to them' (*Investigations* §128)" (1998e, 53).

6.3. The Mental as Such

> What is the natural expression of intention?—Look at a cat when it
> stalks a bird; or a beast when it wants to escape.
>   ((Connexion with propositions about sensations.))   (*PI* §647)

I began the present chapter by calling your attention to the concluding section of "One Strand in the Private Language Argument." There,
McDowell notes that contemporary philosophers of mind tend to split
their subject into two separate problem areas. In one of these, we find
problems about sentience (about sensations, "raw feels," etc.). In the
other lie problems about sapience (about intentionality, propositional
attitudes, thought, etc.). McDowell says that Wittgenstein is "not easy
to place in a landscape organized like this" (1998d, 295), and he observes that, for Wittgenstein, an interest in philosophers' difficulties
with "raw feels" should not be regarded as far removed from an interest in propositional attitudes.

We have now had a chance to see a bit of evidence that supports this
observation. Recall how *PI* §305, whose topic is remembering, helped
us to make sense of §304's discussion of pain. Even though the former
is concerned with sapience and the latter with sentience, as far as
Wittgenstein is concerned, both sections are driving us toward a single
realization. This sort of thing happens often in Wittgenstein's writings.[9] McDowell is right: Wittgenstein doesn't carve up the philosophy of mind as contemporary writers are inclined to. Why is this?
McDowell writes:

> What is striking, in fact, is that in passages like §290 he [Wittgenstein]
> addresses philosophers' difficulties about raw feels with apparatus from
> the sapience part of the supposedly divided subject matter for philoso-
> phy of mind: he talks of language, but my point has been that his
> moves are easily restated in terms of concepts. It is natural to suggest
> that one thing we can learn from Wittgenstein is that there is some-
> thing wrong with the supposed division. Not, of course, that we cannot
> distinguish sapience from sentience; but these are not two simply dif-

9. See, e.g., *PI* §§246–247, where Wittgenstein moves from discussing the sentence
"Only I can know whether I am really in pain" to talking about "Only you can know if
you had that intention."

ferent problem areas—we get into trouble over sentience because we misconceive the role of sapience in constituting our sentient life. Focusing on the ideas that help us to comprehend sapience (centrally the idea of mental life as lived in the space of reasons, that is, the space of concepts) is not, as it sometimes seems, opting to ignore much of what has traditionally counted as philosophy of mind. Perhaps we can even say that Wittgenstein's philosophy of mind can be encapsulated in the remark that mental life is lived in the space of reasons; such a philosophy need not be forgetful of the problem of sentience.   (1998d, 296)

In the first sentence of this passage, McDowell returns to a point made earlier in his paper—that the "moves" made in *PI* §290 are "easily restated in terms of concepts." I have argued, however, that his restatement of these moves distorts their import. Rightly understood, §290 lends no support to the idea that "we get into trouble over sentience because we misconceive the role of sapience in constituting our sentient life." Wittgenstein does not say (or otherwise commit himself to the view) that pains are constituted by the actualization of conceptual capacities. For him, the link between sentience and sapience is not, in this way, a matter of concepts. Still there does appear to be some sort of link. What is it?

*   *   *

It is, I think, a good idea to consider the following questions together:

(1) What has our sentience to do with our sapience?
(2) What does the mental life of a nonlinguistic animal have in common with our sort of mental life?
(3) How are unconscious mental states related to conscious ones?

What's at issue when we consider these questions together is, we might say, the mental as such. And we can approach this issue by noting that the attribution of either a pain or a desire to either a person or a brute is a matter of locating an item in the logical space of animate life. My conscious desire to finish writing this book, my unconscious fear that I'll be punished for any success it brings me, the pain I feel in my wrist when I type too much, my dog's current desire to get outside, and the pain she feels when someone does a poor job of clipping her nails share a kind of intelligibility that the states of hurricanes and hippocampi lack. Part of what this comes to is that all of those mental states may be expressed in behavior. Whether we are talking about sentience or sapience, human beings or brutes, conscious mental states or unconscious ones, the inner and the outer make sense together, in light of each other, in something like the way the words in a sentence make sense together (see §5.3).[10]

According to McDowell's Wittgenstein, mental life is lived in a logical space of *reasons* or, what comes to the same thing for McDowell, a space of *concepts*. But the way in which a pain hangs together with a whimper, in man or beast, is not rational—not a matter of rationally coherent conceptual linkages. This is not to deny that there often *are* rational conceptual linkages between our mental states and their behavioral expressions. Our *actions,* in particular, both express and are rationalized by our attitudes (or better: the *way* in which they are expressed is *rationally*). When I order a pizza, my behavior expresses a belief that helps to rationalize it. But expressive relations between the inner and the outer are not *always* rational relations. If, after an hour of waiting in vain for my spinach and pineapple on whole wheat crust to be delivered, I pound the table in frustration, this behavior expresses my frustration, but it is not rationalized by it.[11]

We *should* avoid the Myth of the Given in our thinking about self-ascriptions of sensation. But we can manage this—indeed, Wittgenstein shows how to manage this—without our having to claim that sensations are constituted by the operations of conceptual capacities. The claim that sensations are so constituted renders problematic not only our relations to our own sensations (as was argued in Chapter 3), but also our kinship with brutes (more on this in a moment). If what I

---

10. I am here stressing what's common between our minds and the minds of brutes. But this is not, of course, to deny that there are major differences. One such difference is hinted at even in this paragraph: although we speak about what animals want, fear, and think, it doesn't make sense to characterize their attitudes or emotions as either conscious or unconscious. (So we don't find ourselves saying things like "Fido *consciously* wanted to go for a run in the park, but *unconsciously* . . ." or "Fifi harbors a great deal of unconscious resentment against. . . .") In §5.3, I argued that what distinguishes a conscious mental state from an unconscious one is a subject's ability to express it merely by avowing it. It makes sense to distinguish between mental states in this way only when one is talking about a creature that lives a linguistic life—a life in which avowals are possible.

11. For more on the connection between expressive and rational relations, see Finkelstein 1999a.

have said in the present chapter is correct, Wittgenstein should not be saddled with any such claim. Better to say that, for him, mental life is lived in the logical space of animate life.

I just indicated that Wittgenstein shows us how we can avoid the Myth of the Given without, as it were, over-rationalizing our inner life. The key is to make the "radical break" called for in *PI* §304, i.e., "to call to mind the differences between the language-games" that are mentioned in §290. We are driven toward the Myth by assuming that whenever someone honestly avows a mental state, he is reporting something that he has learned—something that he would be epistemically justified in affirming. Acknowledging the expressive dimension of these avowals allows us to shed this assumption.

*   *   *

Let's return to our three questions:

(1) What has our sentience to do with our sapience?
(2) What does the mental life of a nonlinguistic animal have in common with our sort of mental life?
(3) How are unconscious mental states related to conscious ones?

A few paragraphs back, I recommended that these questions be looked at together, but it *is* worth our considering how each might be addressed on its own. In §5.4, I talked about how I think Question 3 should be answered. In what follows, I'll say a little bit about how Wittgenstein might address Questions 1 and 2.

Concerning Question 1: Let me call your attention back to a passage from *Zettel* that we looked at in §4.3:

> Plan for the treatment of psychological concepts.
>
> Psychological verbs characterized by the fact that the third person of the present is to be verified by observation, the first person not.
>
> Sentences in the third person of the present: information. In the first person present: expression. ((Not quite right.))
>
> The first person of the present akin to an expression. (*Z* §472; *RPP2* §63)

The phrase "psychological concepts," as used here, refers both to concepts of sentience and sapience. In answer to Question 1, Wittgenstein might point out that our pains and intentions alike exhibit a grammar according to which self-ascriptions of them are, typically, not observation reports, but akin to winces and moans. Typically, when a person speaks about his own pain *or* his own intention, he is not reporting an observed fact but rather expressing—or doing something akin to expressing—the inner state that he is avowing.

Concerning Question 2: I suggested at the end of §6.2 that Wittgenstein isn't the kind of philosopher who will put forward an account of what pain *is*. Instead, he says, in effect, that if you are moved to ask what pain (or fear or joy) is, look to the place that it occupies in our lives:

> The concept of pain is characterized by its particular function in our life.
>
> Pain has *this* position in our life; has *these* connections; (That is to say: we only call "pain" what has *this* position, *these* connexions).
> (*Z* §§532–533)

In answer to Question 2, Wittgenstein might point out that pain occupies a place in the life of a dog or a squirrel that is recognizably akin to the one it occupies in mine. It has a similar function, has some of the same connections. To borrow a useful way of speaking from Diamond (1991),[12] we can see the *face* of pain in the life of a dog or a squirrel—perhaps even in the life of a fly. Wittgenstein writes:

> Look at a stone and imagine it having sensations.—One says to oneself: How could one so much as get the idea of ascribing a *sensation* to a *thing*? One might as well ascribe it to a number!—And now look at a wriggling fly and at once these difficulties vanish and pain seems able to get a foothold here, where before everything was, so to speak, too smooth for it.   (*PI* §284)

None of this is to say that Wittgenstein is committed to some view according to which there is no significant difference between my pain and that of my dog. After all, one way in which my pain may be expressed is via a *conceptual* activity, e.g., an avowal of pain. My pain is situated within a conceptual life; my dog's is not.[13] But we can register

12. See pp. 6, 243–266.

13. Or, if you prefer, my pain is situated within a *fully* conceptual life. I mean to be bracketing the question of whether McDowell is right to deny that nonlinguistic animals have capacities that deserve to be called "conceptual."

this difference without losing our ability to see her pain and mine as the same sort of thing.

Compare what McDowell is in a position to say about the pain of a dog. In answer to Question 2, McDowell, like Wittgenstein, *could* point to the myriad similarities between the place that pain occupies in the life of a dog and the place it occupies in a human life. Nothing prevents him from acknowledging that my behavioral expressions of pain are similar in various ways to my dog's. But in the context of a position according to which my pain just *is* the actualization of conceptual capacities—capacities that my dog entirely lacks—such similarities between my life and hers can't but seem superficial, as if the behavioral overlap in our expressions of pain is akin to the overlap between two quite different diseases both of which happen to produce, say, an itchy rash as a symptom. The middle path account of inner awareness induces an inability to see the face of pain in the life of an animal (i.e., an inability to see an animal's expressions of pain *as* expressions of pain). What Wittgenstein has to say about self-ascriptions of pain does not.

*   *   *

In the opening chapter of his *Philosophy and the Mirror of Nature,* Richard Rorty writes:

> The obvious objection to defining the mental as the intentional is that pains are not intentional—they do not represent, they are not *about* anything. The obvious objection to defining the mental as "the phenomenal" is that beliefs don't feel like anything—they don't have phenomenal properties, and a person's real beliefs are not always what they appear to be. The attempt to hitch pains and beliefs together seems ad hoc—they don't seem to have anything in common except our refusal to call them "physical."   (Rorty 1979, 22)

What ought we to say about this passage? McDowell says, in effect, that pains and beliefs have more in common than is suggested here: they share a kind of intelligibility. To understand someone either as feeling a pain or as holding a particular belief is to situate items in "a logical space that is *sui generis,* by comparison with the realm of [natural] law" (McDowell 1996, 72), i.e., it is to make things intelligible in a way that the natural sciences do not. This seems to me the right approach toward answering the challenge posed by the passage from Rorty. But, for McDowell, coming to see that this *is* the right approach must be, in part, a matter of bringing oneself to deny what is, according to the first sentence of the quotation, "[t]he obvious objection to defining the mental as the intentional": one must maintain that pains *represent*— that the pain in my wrist is about something, namely itself.

The picture of mind that emerges in McDowell's remarks about inner awareness is one according to which our attitudes and sensations alike are wholly conceptual affairs; they are constituted by the operations of conceptual capacities. In Chapter 3, I argued that this picture misrepresents our experience of sensations. In the present chapter, I have urged that it leaves too little room for our sense of ourselves as not wholly disconnected from animals—our sense that they, like us, enjoy and suffer sentience. I have, moreover, argued that McDowell misascribes it to Wittgenstein.

As I have suggested that he be read, Wittgenstein shows how we can embrace the idea that pains and beliefs share a kind of intelligibility, without our having to claim that the former are *about* anything, without our having to distance human sentience so much from that of brutes that we are unable to continue seeing the latter as genuinely sentient at all, and without our subscribing to the Myth of the Given either. Paying the right sort of attention to what Wittgenstein has to say about expression and the expressive dimension of mental state self-ascriptions can help us to think about not only first-person authority and consciousness, but also the mental as such.

6.4. Self-*Knowledge*?

I've suggested at several points in this chapter that we ought to avoid the Myth of the Given—not as McDowell does, by understanding our pains to have propositional content, but by rejecting the idea that self-ascriptions of pain are, as a rule, epistemically justified. Perhaps I've made doing this sound easier than it is. Consider the following objection to my suggestion: "Suppose Hank reads in a medical journal that someone who gets a sharp pain in the back of his knee is more likely than the average American to get Green's disease. At some point thereafter, Hank experiences just such a pain and infers that he's more likely than the average American to get Green's disease. At this point, Hank is justified in believing that he's more likely than the average American to get the disease. But he couldn't be justified in believing this—the *conclusion* of his inference—if he were not justified in believing the premises, one of which is that he has a sharp pain in the back of his knee. In order for Hank to have gotten himself into the epistemic position that he's now in, he must have judged that he has a pain in the back of his knee or, anyway, ascribed such a pain to himself, and he must have been epistemically justified in so doing. Moreover, there's nothing extraordinary about this self-ascription of Hank's. Our self-ascriptions of pain and other mental states just *are* available to figure as grounds when we make inferences. Thus they must, in general, be epistemically justified."

The right reply to this argument is, I think, to deny its central presupposition, viz., that whenever someone comes to be justified in believing something by virtue of making an inference from a number of premises, he must be epistemically justified in believing (or would be so justified in asserting) all of the premises. In §6.1, I discussed Wittgenstein's saying, "To use a word without justification does not mean to use it without right" (*PI* §289). I would urge that when Hank infers that he is more likely than the average American to get Green's disease, he is using a statement about his pain—as a premise—without epistemic justification but not without right.[14]

But now, am *I* subscribing to the Myth of the Given? After all, I'm allowing that Hank's self-ascription of pain is an unjustified justifier. But the Myth of the Given is not the idea that justifications come to an end somewhere. One subscribes to the Myth if one claims that something (some state or episode or whatever) without conceptual content available to a subject is, nonetheless, the subject's ground (or justification or reason) for believing (or judging or asserting) that such-and-such. I

---

14. I should say, however, that I would have no serious objection to someone's using the words "with justification" in the way that I'm using "not without right." In that case, to say that someone was *justified* in self-ascribing a pain would not imply that he was *basing* his self-ascription on anything (e.g., the pain or an observation of it). The point is not to insist on this or that way of speaking, but to avoid philosophical confusion.

am claiming no such thing. On the view that I'm recommending, Hank's judgment that he is likely to get Green's disease is the conclusion of an inference, one of whose premises is a fully conceptual self-ascription of pain. There *is* a sense in which this self-ascription could be described as *given:* Hank doesn't need an epistemic justification—he doesn't need to find out that he's in pain, or to be under the impression that he is—in order to be, so to speak, *entitled* to ascribe pain to himself. But I've argued, in effect, that there is nothing problematic about something's being given in this way.[15]

*   *   *

At this point, the following question might be put to me: "On your view, does Hank *know* that he has a sharp pain in the back of his knee? If his self-ascription of pain is not epistemically justified, this suggests that he shouldn't be said to know. On the other hand, imagine that two people are discussing how it is that Hank knows about his increased likelihood of getting Green's disease. Couldn't one of them

15. What I've said in this paragraph might suggest to some readers that I mean to be taking Davidson's side against the account of *outer* experience that McDowell defends in *Mind and World*. (For a very brief discussion of McDowell's disagreement with Davidson, see §3.1.) In fact, I'm not, in this book, committing myself one way or the other on the question of how we should think about outer, perceptual experience. If I say that *pains* have no propositional content, this is not to say that perceptual experiences also lack such content. On my view, it is a mistake to think of pains as perceptual experiences (or as very much like them). It would be perfectly consistent with what I'm saying here about pains to hold, *with* McDowell, that when someone sees, and so comes to believe, that there's a pencil on her desk, her belief is justified by a conceptual visual impression to the effect that there's a pencil on her desk. Indeed, it is arguable that this central commitment of *Mind and World* is rendered *more* attractive if it is divorced from the middle path account of inner awareness. Even setting aside the objection I adduced against the middle path account in Chapter 3, it is *prima facie* much more plausible to claim that outer, perceptual experience has propositional content (to say, e.g., that I'm right now under the visual impression that there is a dog on the floor to my right) than to say that pains have such content (to say, e.g., that my headache is to the effect that I have a headache). The position I have been defending in this book shows how it might be possible to retain the former, plausible claim while giving up the latter, implausible one.

say: 'He knows *both* that anyone who has a sharp pain in the back of the knee is likely to get the disease *and* that he has a sharp pain in the back of the knee. So he's made the obvious inference'?"

A famous passage from the *Investigations* runs as follows:

> In what sense are my sensations *private?*—Well, only I can know whether I am really in pain; another person can only surmise it.—In one way this is wrong, and in another nonsense. If we are using the word "to know" as it is normally used (and how else are we to use it?), then other people very often know when I am in pain.—Yes, but all the same not with the certainty with which I know it myself!—It can't be said of me at all (except perhaps as a joke) that I *know* I am in pain. What is it supposed to mean—except perhaps that I *am* in pain? (*PI* §246)

The point here is not to insist that one could never make good use of the words "I know I am in pain." One might use them in a joke. And the final quoted sentence suggests that one *might* use these words to mean the same thing that's usually meant by "I *am* in pain."

Someone *could* say (meaningfully, truly) of Hank: "He knows *both* that anyone who has a sharp pain in the back of the knee is likely to get the disease *and* that he has a sharp pain in the back of the knee. So he's made the obvious inference." But one might *just as well* say: "He knows that anyone who has a sharp pain in the back of the knee is likely to get the disease, and he *has* a sharp pain in the back of the knee. So he's made the obvious inference." What's important is that we not take the possibility of employing the first formulation instead of the second to imply that Hank's "self-knowledge" is of a piece with someone's knowing that he has termites in his basement.

Imagine three philosophers who are talking about Hank's case. The first says: "Hank has a sharp pain in the back of his knee, but it's wrong to speak of him as either *knowing* or *not knowing* about it. Such talk is, at best, unnatural and misleading and, at worst, sheer nonsense." The second philosopher says: "Hank has ascribed a pain to himself, and he is entitled to make inferences on the basis of this self-ascription. But such an ascription of pain is not epistemically justified; he *doesn't know* that he's in pain." The third says: "Hank *does* knows that he's in pain; we *can* say this about him. The mistake is to think that knowledge always requires epistemic justification. He knows that he's in pain, but knowing this isn't like knowing that one has termites in one's basement." I don't see that these philosophers need be disagreeing about anything of genuine philosophical import. Moreover, it seems to me that all three of them might agree with everything I've said in this book.

Deliberation and Transparency

At the end of Chapter 2, I argued that constitutivism is bound to represent us as responsible for our own inner states in ways that we are not. This problem, you may recall, is more apparent when we consider the authority with which a person says, "I have a headache," than when we think about someone's speaking about his own attitudes. A constitutivist account of the self-ascription of pain has very little *prima facie* appeal. But because we are responsible for, e.g., our intentions, it does not seem an obviously bad idea to claim that first-person authority about them derives from the fact that they are somehow constituted by what we think or say about them. The problem with this suggestion (we saw) is that the responsibility we bear for what we intend is different in character from the responsibility we bear for what we say or believe about our intentions. (Thus a person may be admired for his honesty in avowing an intention while being blamed for having the intention.)

That we are responsible for our intentions at all is not unrelated to the fact that we are able to reflect on them deliberatively and decide what to do. Richard Moran's recent *Authority and Estrangement* may be understood as an attempt to take seriously—more seriously than a constitutivist is in a position to—this kind of deliberative reflection and to explain thereby the authority with which we speak not only about our own intentions but about our desires, beliefs, fears, and other attitudes as well. Moran's position is neither a version of constitutivism nor a middle path between constitutivism and detectivism. While both Wright and McDowell could be described as holding that our mental states are often constituted by awarenesses of them, this would not be an apt description of Moran. Nonetheless, Moran aims to show that what explains self-knowledge and first-person authority is the fact that a subject gets to make up her own mind about what she intends, wants, believes, etc. The result is an account of inner awareness that is, in the terms I used in the introduction to Chapter 3, strong on intimacy, naturalness, and responsibility, but immune to the difficulties that come with claiming that mental states and events are constituted by awarenesses of them.

There is much in *Authority and Estrangement* that I admire and agree with. For example, Moran is struck by the fact that a person might find out about one of her own unconscious mental states without the state's thereby becoming conscious, and he sees that this fact makes trouble for detectivism. Moreover, he suggests that a commitment to either detectivism or constitutivism precludes one from appreciating what is, as it were, first-personal about a subject's relations to her own mental states. Thus, he writes:

> One thing that is unsatisfying about any perceptual model of self-consciousness is that perception is a relation that, in principle, should be possible with respect to a whole range of a phenomena of a certain type. On such a model, then, there would seem to be no deep reason why one couldn't bear this quasi-perceptual relation to the mental life of another person as well as oneself.   (Moran 2001, 33; also see p. 25, where a related complaint is stated about Crispin Wright's constitutivism.)

I read Moran's book after mine was completed, and, rather than try to weave a discussion of it into a finished manuscript, I'm going to say a little bit here both about it and about the approach toward understanding self-knowledge and first-person authority that it may be understood to represent. (As we'll see, Gareth Evans and Sydney Shoemaker share this approach.)[1]

*   *   *

1. I'm indebted to Shadi Bartsch, Jim Conant, Cora Diamond, Jay Elliott, Jennifer Hornsby, Ben McMyler, and Michael Morgan for their comments on a draft of this Postscript. Most of what's presented here was presented in a graduate seminar that I taught at the University of Chicago in the spring of 2003 on self-knowledge and first-person authority. I'm grateful to the seminar participants.

Let's begin with a passage from Evans's *Varieties of Reference* that is quoted approvingly by Moran:

> [I]n making a self-ascription of belief, one's eyes are, so to speak, or oc-
> casionally literally, directed outward—upon the world. If someone asks
> me "Do you think there is going to be a third world war?", I must at-
> tend, in answering him, to precisely the same outward phenomena as I
> would attend to if I were answering the question "Will there be a third
> world war?"   (Evans 1982, 225; quoted in Moran 2001, 61)

If I am asked whether I believe it will rain, I look *up* at the sky. I don't look *inward* to the contents of my own mind (or to my own behavior). When I say what I believe, I'm not reporting a self-observation. The point is sometimes put (e.g., by Moran) in terms of the "transparency" of one question to another: for me, the question of whether or not I believe that p is transparent to the question of whether or not p is true. I answer the former question by doing what I would do in order to an-swer the latter. Thus, the quoted passage continues: "I get myself in a position to answer the question whether I believe that p by putting into operation whatever procedure I have for answering the question whether p" (Evans 1982, 225).

We can distinguish two kinds of reaction to this point about the self-ascription of belief: call them "Very Impressed" and "Not So Im-pressed." A Very Impressed reaction would be to conclude that belief self-ascription, understood in terms of transparency, provides a model —a rough model, perhaps, but a good one nonetheless—for explain-ing how we manage to speak with authority about a wide range of our own inner states and goings on. A philosopher who is Very Impressed by transparency is likely to say that if we hope to understand the phe-nomenon of first-person authority, *this* is where we should begin—with the transparency of belief self-ascriptions to outward-looking questions about the world. A philosopher who is Not So Impressed will probably hold that this transparency is not going to generalize in such a way as to provide the key to understanding the self-ascription of very much besides belief. Thus a Not So Impressed *detectivist* might say: "If we spoke with first-person authority only about our own current beliefs, then perhaps there would be no purpose in positing an inner sense. But we speak with authority about our own fear, desire, revulsion, pain, joy, hatred, and past belief, among other things. The question of what it is that I want or fear or adore is *not* transparent to any question about the outer world. In order to answer such a question, I must look inward, and to accomplish this, I need an inner sense."

I take it that Evans, Shoemaker, and Moran are all Very Impressed by transparency. Of the three, Evans does the least to show that *we* ought to be Very Impressed as well,[2] and I won't say any more about him here. I won't say much about Shoemaker either, but I do want to dwell for a moment on one attempt he makes to extend the point about transparency beyond belief to desire—if only to bring out that this is not an easy thing to do successfully.

In a number of papers,[3] Shoemaker argues against the idea of inner sense by trying to show that a person's being rational, coupled with her enjoying normal conceptual capacities, suffices to provide her with normal self-awareness; there is no need to posit an inner sense in order to account for self-knowledge or first-person authority. Shoemaker's argumentative strategy is to have us *try* to imagine a rational agent with normal conceptual capacities whose mechanism of inner sense has broken down—someone who might be described as "self-blind." He reasons that if self-knowledge comes by way of an inner sense, we should at least be able to conceive of a person who is damaged in this way. Moreover, such a person should exhibit a *deficit* of some kind. But, according to Shoemaker, when we try to imagine a self-blind person, we find ourselves imagining someone who exhibits normal self-awareness. Self-blindness, in other words, turns out to be unimaginable.

The argument begins with Shoemaker's pointing out that our (so-called) self-blind person won't exhibit any deficit when she is asked whether or not she believes that *p*—for a rational agent with normal conceptual capacities "will answer affirmatively to the question 'Do you believe that P?' if and only if she will answer affirmatively to the question 'Is it true that P?'" (Shoemaker 1994, 282). Here, Shoemaker appeals, in effect, to the transparency of belief self-ascription. So far so good, perhaps, but he needs to show that normal rationality and conceptual capacities suffice not only for ordinary self-awareness of *belief*

2. I don't mean to be faulting Evans; his discussion of mental state self-ascription is a kind of *aside* in *The Varieties of Reference*—one that he introduces by saying, "My discussion of the ways in which we have knowledge of our own *mental* states will be extremely incomplete" (1982, 224).

3. See, e.g., Shoemaker 1988 and Shoemaker 1994.

but for ordinary self-awareness of other mental states as well. Thus, after arguing that we cannot imagine a rational agent who is self-blind to belief, he writes:

> Similar remarks apply to desire. The rational agent who wants X and has normal mastery of language will, ceteris paribus, respond affirmatively to the question "Shall I give you X?" And given her mastery of the concept of desire, she will respond affirmatively to the question "Do you want X?" if she will respond affirmatively to the question "Shall I give you X?" So she will, unless she has devious motives, give correct answers to questions about what she wants.   (1994, 283)

We can understand this passage as attempting to extend the point about transparency to desire. According to Shoemaker, a rational agent should answer the question of whether or not she wants X not by considering *herself* but by considering *X*—by doing what she would do if she were asked, "Shall I give you X?" If this is correct, then neither in the case of belief nor in the case of desire does self-awareness require that one look *inward*. One can ascribe beliefs and desires to oneself by engaging with questions that make no reference to *inner* states or events.

A bit of reflection on the quoted passage, however, suggests an obvious difficulty for this line of thought: There needn't be anything irrational in someone's uttering a sentence of the form "I want X, but I don't want you to give it to me." ("I want that car, but I don't want anyone to buy it for me; I'm going to earn the money for it myself." "I want a good term paper topic, but I don't want you to just give me one.") Moreover, some of the things that we want cannot be passed from one person to another. I might ask you whether you want a solitary life of quiet contemplation. Your answering this question would not be a matter of your responding as you would (presumably with some puzzlement) if I were to say, "Shall I give you a solitary life of quiet contemplation?" The connection between "Do you want X?" and "Shall I give you X?" is just nowhere near as tight as that between "Do you believe that p?" and "Is p true?"

Could this worry be addressed by substituting another question (or set of questions) for Shoemaker's "Shall I give you X?" It's far from obvious that it could be. Consider, for example, "Would you have X?" While it is, perhaps, difficult to think of situations in which one would be moved to utter a sentence of the form "I want X, but I wouldn't have it," it does not seem as if substituting "Would you have X?" for "Shall I give you X?" in Shoemaker's argument would make it more convincing. For so doing would only suggest another worry: Why should we think that answering a question of the form "Would you have X?" does not require that one look *inward*? Why, for that matter, should we think that answering a question of the form "Shall I give you X?" doesn't often call for one to look inward?

It seems compelling to claim, against the detectivist, both (1) that when I say whether I *believe*, e.g., it's going to rain, I am drawing on the same perceptual and conceptual capacities as when I say whether it *is* going to rain *and* (2) that the exercise of these capacities requires no mechanism of *inner* sense. But finding a way to make an equally compelling pair of parallel claims when what's at issue is desire, rather than belief, is something that I don't believe Shoemaker ever manages. Moreover, the task would only become harder if he were to shift his attention from belief and desire to, say, regret or loathing.

I won't say any more here about Shoemaker's argument against inner sense. My present aim is not to provide a detailed criticism of this argument;[4] I mean only to be gesturing toward the kind of difficulties that arise when one takes the avowal of belief to be the paradigm case of mental state self-ascription. It's not *easy*, anyway, to show that we should be Very Impressed by transparency. In what remains of this postscript, I'll be focusing on Moran's Very Impressed account of self-knowledge and first-person authority.

*   *   *

Early on in *Authority and Estrangement,* Moran writes:

> There are two basic categories of psychological state to which the ordinary assumption of "privileged access" is meant to apply: occurrent states such as sensations and passing thoughts, and various standing attitudes of the person, such as beliefs, emotional attitudes, and intentions. (I will have comparatively little to say here about the case of sensations, which I believe raises issues for self-knowledge quite different from the case of attitudes of various kinds.)   (Moran 2001, 9–10)

4. This *is* my aim in Finkelstein 1999b.

Moran means to account for "the case of attitudes" only; he is not trying to explain the access we have to, or the authority with which we speak about, our own sensations or passing thoughts.[5] Still, we speak with first-person authority about a wide range of attitudes. How, according to Moran, should we understand our "privileged access" to them?

Like Evans and Shoemaker, Moran is struck by the fact that the question of what it is that I believe is, for me, transparent to the question of what is in fact the case. He argues that what accounts for this feature of belief self-ascription is that I approach the question of what I believe in what he calls a "deliberative," rather than a "theoretical," spirit. I don't ask, "What is it that this person, who happens to be me, believes? What is his psychological condition?" Rather, I ask myself what *to* believe:

> [T]he vehicle of transparency . . . lies in the requirement that I address myself to the question of my state of mind in a *deliberative* spirit, deciding and declaring myself on the matter, and not confront the question as a purely psychological one about the beliefs of someone who happens also to be me.   (2001, 63)

In order to address, in a deliberative spirit, the question of whether or not I believe it will rain, I must be sensitive to the reasons for and against *believing that it will rain*—not the reasons for and against *believing that someone believes it will rain*.

According to Moran, it is not only the question of whether or not I believe some claim that may be approached in this spirit. If you ask me whether I fear X, I will, probably, consider whether or not I ought to fear it. I will take account of—not the reasons for thinking that a particular person is afraid of X, but—the reasons for being afraid of it. I'll reflect (to the extent that I do reflect) on X, not on myself. I'll consider not my fear but its object. (Is it dangerous? Is it liable to do me harm?)[6] Now let's say that I come, in this way, to realize that I ought

---

5. In this, he is like Crispin Wright (see Chapter 2).

6. Deliberatively addressing the question of whether or not I fear X requires more than that I assess the practical reasons for and against fearing X. I must assess them with an eye toward making up my mind about whether *to* fear X. Thus Moran writes:

to fear X or intend Y. *If* there is no further question for me about whether I do in fact fear X or intend Y—if I am able, simply on the basis of assessing the practical reasons, to say that I fear X or intend Y—then, in Moran's terms, the "Transparency Condition" is met, and my statement counts as an "avowal." Thus, I avow my fear in this sense[7] not by looking inward but by attending to the object of my fear. Moran thinks that this is what ordinarily occurs when we speak about our own attitudes: "in ordinary circumstances a claim concerning one's attitudes counts as a claim about their objects, about the world one's attitudes are directed upon" (2001, 92).

Moran acknowledges that avowal is not always possible; the Transparency Condition is not always met. I may find myself fearing something that I don't take myself to have good reason to fear, or intending to do something that I know I ought not to do. In such a circumstance, I might report my attitude, but I could not avow it. According to Moran, such cases must be exceptional:

> In a certain case, I may see how all the evidence points to a conclusion I cannot bring myself to believe, or I may reason my way to a conclusion about what to do that leaves me with a further task of somehow managing to commit myself to it. . . . In what must be the standard situation of deliberation, however, the person's conclusion *is* his belief or intention, not something that he now needs to find a way to impose upon himself. Here he is not "working on" his states of mind, the way he might with respect to another person, nor is he trying to produce results in himself. If he were, then he would indeed need to "see" what the states of mind are that he is trying to manipulate, the way the akratic person relates to his desire. Rather, in conceiving of the ques-

---

"The idea of 'deliberative' reflection about one's response is meant to denote something more than simply the normative appraisal of it, the sort of reflection that would terminate in some settled assessment of it. For the mere appraisal of one's attitudes, however normative, would apply equally well to past as well as to current attitudes and indeed may have just the same application to another person as to oneself. In itself, such assessment is not a first-person affair. Rather, 'deliberative' reflection as intended here is of the same family of thought as practical reflection, which does not conclude with normative judgment *about* what would be best to do, but with the formation of an actual intention *to do* something" (2001, 59).

7. In what follows, I'll try to use the word "avow" in Moran's specialized sense. This was, of course, not my practice in the chapters preceding this Postscript.

tions hc's asking as part of the specific activity of deliberating, he has asserted the determination of the answer by justifying reasons rather than explanatory ones.   (2001, 131–132)

When I avow an intention to do something, it's as if the reasons for doing it speak *through* me; I've bound myself to them, and now I intend whatever course of action they dictate: "To engage in deliberation in the first place is to hand over the question of one's belief or intentional action to the authority of reason" (2001, 127).

Moran describes himself as arguing "the case for seeing the ability to avow one's belief as the fundamental form of self-knowledge, one that gives proper place to the immediacy of first-person awareness and the authority with which its claims are delivered" (2001, 150). He holds that first-person authority is explained by the fact that often I am able to settle the question of whether I believe, intend, desire, or fear something by reflecting deliberatively on whether I ought to and avowing my state of mind, i.e., declaring myself one way or the other, just as the reasons dictate.

As we found in our discussion of Shoemaker, it is difficult to claim that the self-ascription of belief provides a model of self-knowledge that can be used in order to understand our awareness of our own, say, desires because there seems to be no "outward-directed" question that bears the kind of relation to "Do I want X?" that the question "Is it the case that *p*?" bears to "Do I believe that *p*?" Moran argues, in effect, that the question "Ought I to want X?" can be such a question—*when* the Transparency Condition is met, when a person manages to tie herself, as it were, to the mast of practical reason.[8] One who has managed this comes to know what she wants simply by determining what she ought to want, i.e., what the reasons speak in favor of her wanting. Thus Moran makes his case for our being Very Impressed by transparency.

*   *   *

Should we be Very Impressed? Have we been offered a satisfactory account of self-knowledge or first-person authority? According to

---

8. I *might* address the question of what I ought to want as a merely theoretical inquiry—the way I might address the question of what you ought to want. In such a case, the Transparency Condition would not be met.

Moran, "The conclusion to be secured by these [his] considerations is that avowal is indeed a vehicle of self-knowledge, and that it is what makes the difference between genuine first-person awareness and a purely theoretical or attributional knowledge of one's states" (2001, 107). One very serious obstacle to accepting this conclusion is that we speak with first-person authority about a great many mental states and events that are not avowable in Moran's sense. Let's consider some of them.

There are, of course, sensations and other occurrent mental goings-on, which Moran acknowledges from the start that he does not mean to be speaking about. If I say, "My head hurts," I'm not declaring the answer to any deliberative question.

There are all of our *past* mental states. Given Moran's position, if, speaking honestly, I say upon your late arrival to an engagement, "I was worried about you," I do not thereby exhibit "genuine first-person awareness" because I am not addressing the question of what *to* worry about—only the question of what I did in fact worry about. (I am not, in other words, addressing any question in a deliberative spirit.)[9] Nonetheless, as with sensations, it seems as if we often do speak with first-person authority about past mental states.

There are the attitudes that I cannot avow because the reasons speak against them. Moran notes that "I may confess that my fear is beyond my control, and that I can't help being afraid of something, where, by my own lights, there is nothing to be feared" (2001, 63). He doesn't say how we are able to speak about such fears with first-person authority. But of course we do. If, on some occasion when I've been called upon to speak in public or to pick up a snake, you want to know whether I'm afraid, I am the best person to ask. And I am able to say whether I'm afraid without considering, or needing to consider, evidence, regardless of whether I take fear to be a *reasonable* response to my situation. According to Moran, "A proper philosophical account of self-knowledge should tell us how it is that a person can speak about his own mind, without appealing to evidence about himself," where his not appealing to evidence "contributes rather than detracts from the authority of what he says" (2001, 135). I enjoy this sort of "knowledge"

---

9. See the passage quoted in n. 6. While I *can* ask myself whether some past attitude of mine was warranted, this is not "deliberation."

about attitudes that are, according to my own assessment, irrational, and so, on Moran's account, unavowable.[10]

The last class of mental states about which we speak with first-person authority despite the fact that they cannot be, in Moran's sense, avowed is quite large. I have in mind all the attitudes that would be neither prohibited nor required by deliberative reflection. One kind of example is presented by such states of mind as disdain, adoration, jealousy, regret, revulsion, and hatred. What these and other attitudes have in common is that, even though we sometimes deliberate about their appropriateness, they are rarely thought to be *required* by practical reasons. A friend might try to convince me that it's unreasonable for me to adore a dog who is continually leaving teeth-marks on my furniture. But when a dog behaves well, I'm under no rational obligation to adore him, and when I declare that I adore *my* dog, I am not merely articulating the conclusion of some bit of (explicit or implicit) practical reasoning. The authority of such a self-ascription cannot be explained by claiming that I've let the practical reasons take me where they will.

Another kind of example is presented by what we might call brute likes and dislikes. So: I dislike goat cheese intensely. But I don't believe goat cheese to be bad or undesirable or something that one ought not to like. I understand that fine people of excellent taste love the stuff. Thus, on the one hand, I'm not being moved by practical reasons to dislike goat cheese. On the other hand, my disliking it doesn't mean that I'm being unreasonable or irrational. The practical reasons leave me a bit of latitude here.

I believe that the closest Moran comes to speaking about brute likes and dislikes is when he says the following about brute *desires:*

> Some desires, such as those associated with hunger or sheer fatigue, may be experienced by the person as feelings that simply come over him. They simply happen. On some occasions their occurrence may be inexplicable to him, and their inexplicability in such cases need not di-

---

10. Sometimes a person is drawn to an activity in part *because* it is unreasonable. We can imagine someone—a rebellious teenager, perhaps—who is planning (perhaps carefully planning) to do something that is, by his own or anyone's lights, practically unreasonable. Such a person is not barred from speaking with first-person authority about his intention to do whatever crazy thing he's planning to do.

minish their force. Like an alien intruder, they must simply be re-
sponded to, even if one doesn't understand what they're doing there
or what the sense of their demands is. The person's stance toward such
desires, and how he deals with them, may be little different from his
stance toward any other empirical phenomenon he confronts. From
this angle, a brute desire is a bit of reality for the agent to accommodate, like a sensation, or a broken leg, or an obstacle in one's path.
(2001, 114–115)

Pace Moran, my relation to a brute desire for a snack (or, for that matter, to one of my sensations—notice the reference to sensation in the
last sentence of the quoted passage), like my relation to my attitude toward goat cheese, is *very* different from my relation to an obstacle in
my path. I speak with first-person authority about brute desires and
brute dislikes. I enjoy a first-personal relation to my conscious desires
and dislikes whether or not they are avowable in Moran's sense. But
because Moran understands "the ability to avow one's belief as the fundamental form of self-knowledge, one that gives proper place to the
immediacy of first-person awareness and the authority with which its
claims are delivered" [2001, 134])—because he, in effect, explains
first-person authority *as* avowability—this is not a point that he's in a
position to accommodate.

What's starting to emerge is that Moran often speaks as if there are
just two boxes into which our states of mind may be understood to belong: one containing "avowable" attitudes, attitudes that could be the
conclusions of deliberations under the Transparency Condition, and
the other containing attitudes to which we don't bear genuine first-
personal relations. In this vein, he writes:

[W]ith respect to one's emotional life, a person may want to know what
his true feelings about something are, or he may be engaged in making
up his mind, coming to some settled response he can respect, or at
least make sense of; that is, his inquiry may be either a purely theoretical one about his psychological state as it is, or part of the process of
forming his feelings.

What we're calling a theoretical question about oneself, then, is one
that is answered by discovery of the fact of which one was ignorant,
whereas a practical or deliberative question is answered by a decision
or commitment of some sort, and it is not a response to ignorance of
some antecedent fact about oneself.   (2001, 58)

But when I tell you that I dislike goat cheese (or that I was worried about you before you finally arrived), I am neither addressing a deliberative question nor responding to *ignorance* of some fact about myself. I am speaking with first-person authority even though I am not, in Moran's sense, avowing anything.

According to Moran, "avowal . . . is what makes the difference between genuine first-person awareness and a purely theoretical or attributional knowledge of one's states" (2001, 107), and "attributional self-knowledge . . . is the expression of an essentially third-personal stance toward oneself" (2001, 106). Because avowal, as he understands it, is so often impossible, these remarks imply that our awareness of *many* of our own conscious attitudes (e.g., my awareness that I adore my dog) is essentially third-personal—akin, in other words, to a person's perceptual awareness that an obstacle lies in his path. Thus, in spite of Moran's opposition to detectivism, his account of self-knowledge leads back to it.[11]

*   *   *

I have been focusing on cases in which we speak with first-person authority about our states of mind even though we are not in a position to do what Moran calls avowing them. But what about the cases in which we do seem to avow attitudes? Imagine that Max and Sarah are examining the rather limited menu at a small French restaurant when Sarah asks Max what he intends to order. He deliberates: he first rules out most of the items on the menu because they contain beef, chicken, or pork, and he judges it morally wrong to eat these things. He then eliminates several other dishes because, appealing as they are to him, they contain a lot of fat, and his doctor has told him that he should cut down on fat. It turns out that this leaves him with just one option—the salad niçoise. He answers, "I intend to order the salad niçoise; how about you?"

This is an ideal case for Moran. According to his account (as I understand it), Max's avowal of intention is the conclusion of a bit of

---

11. A lesson of Wittgenstein's: freeing one's thinking from the distortions imposed on it by detectivism (where this does not mean merely recoiling from detectivism toward a position according to which what we say about our own fears and intentions fails to reflect what we fear and intend) is hard to do. I don't believe that Wright, McDowell, or Moran manages it. The "radical break" called for in *PI* §304 doesn't come easily (see §6.2 above).

practical deliberation. Because he has succeeded in effectively committing himself to order whatever the practical reasons speak in favor of his ordering, the question of what he intends (or *wants,* in one sense of this word)[12] to order is, for him, transparent to the question of what he should order. He thus comes to know what he intends simply by deliberating about these reasons and arriving at a conclusion about what to do. When he says, "I intend to order the salad niçoise," his first-person authority comes to this: he is stating a conclusion at which he's arrived, not by looking "inward" to the contents of his own mind but by an "outward-looking" consideration of the reasons for and against ordering the various items on the menu.

If we consider only this case, the explanation of it just given sounds quite good. Moran's is the most sophisticated attempt of which I'm aware to understand self-knowledge and first-person authority in terms of transparency. He shows that sometimes the question of what a person intends, wants, or fears is, for him, transparent to the question of what he ought to do or to fear. Moran succeeds, that is, in extending the point about transparency *beyond* belief.[13] Nonetheless, it is striking

---

12. There is a kind of (non-appetitive) wanting that always accompanies intending. Michael Thompson brings this out by noting that whenever someone says that he is doing A with the intention of doing B, it makes sense to reply, "And why do you want to do B?" (Thompson, n.d., 14–15).

13. This makes things sound simpler than they are. In fact, there are *two* points about transparency and belief that haven't yet been distinguished at all clearly: (1) Whether or not someone consciously believes that p is, for her, (always) transparent to the question of whether or not p is true. And (2) when (and only when) the Transparency Condition is met, the question of whether or not someone believes that p is, for her, transparent to the question of whether or not she has good reason to believe that p. What Moran shows, it seems to me, is that point (2) can be extended to attitudes other than belief. He shows, e.g., that when (and only when) the Transparency Condition is met, whether someone fears that p is, for her, transparent to the question of whether she has good reason to fear that p. It's worth noting, however, that *this* kind of transparency is absent when someone consciously *believes* something that she knows it is not reasonable to believe. So consider the case of Lana: She is married to a Marine who has been missing in action for years. Lana understands that all the evidence points to his being dead, but she can't bring herself to believe that he is. If she is asked about her husband, she's liable to say something like, "I believe he's alive, even though I know it's unreasonable of me not to think him dead." For Lana, the question of whether she *believes* her husband is alive is *not* transparent to the question of whether she has *good reason* to believe that he's alive. But, for her, the former

how limited this extension turns out to be. Surely, a satisfactory account of self-knowledge or first-person authority—indeed a satisfactory account even of Max's authority when he says what he intends to order—should help us to understand what the case just described (call it "case 1") has in common with the following variations on it:

Case 2. On looking over the menu, Max concludes that he ought to order the salad niçoise for the reasons outlined above. But he neither forms nor avows an intention to do so. He answers Sarah's question—"What do you intend to order?"—as follows: "Ravioli with wild mushroom sauce. I know I should order the salad, but I'm not going to."

Case 3. Max rules out the beef, pork, and chicken because he thinks it's wrong to eat them, and he eliminates the items that contain a lot of fat because of what his doctor has said. This leaves him two options: the salad niçoise and a salad that features (low-fat) goat cheese. He rules out the latter because he happens not to like goat cheese, and he says, "I intend to order the salad niçoise."

Case 4. Max and Sarah are looking over the menu at a restaurant where they dine frequently. Max usually orders either the salad niçoise or the halibut. He enjoys both, and both strike him as healthy choices. On looking over the menu, he concludes, as usual, that he ought to order either the salad niçoise or the halibut. When Sarah asks him what he intends to order, he answers, "Salad niçoise." If she were to ask, "Why not the halibut?" he would reply, "I'm just in the mood for salad niçoise."

Max speaks with first-person authority in each of these cases. And at this point, I hope it's clear why each poses a problem for Moran: In case 2, Max's statement about his intention goes against his own assessment of what he ought to do. In case 3, Max's first-person "access" to one of the reasons that figures in his deliberating seems, on Moran's

question *is* transparent to that of whether husband is, in fact, alive. (She would not say, "I believe that he is alive, even though he is, in fact, not.") It is *because* Moran, in effect, focuses on the second point about transparency—on point (2) rather than point (1)—that his account of self-knowledge and first-person authority *can* be extended to cases involving attitudes other than belief but *cannot* be extended to *all* cases in which someone speaks about a conscious belief with first-person authority.

account, inexplicable. Lastly, Moran's account would suggest that in case 4, Max should be able to declare with first-person authority that he intends to order *either* the salad niçoise or the halibut, but he should not be able to say with first-person authority *which* of the two he intends to order.

I have tried in the chapters preceding this postscript to offer an account of psychological self-ascription that enables us to see what it is that's present in cases 1 through 4 but absent when Max speaks about an unconscious attitude or an obstacle in his path. In cases 1 through 4, Max's self-ascription of intention, his assertion (and it *is* an assertion) that he intends to order this or that, is an *expression* of his intention. He expresses his intention by ascribing it to himself. By contrast, if Max were to ascribe an *unconscious* attitude to himself—if, e.g., he were to say, "I keep eating your ravioli because I unconsciously want to gain weight"—he would not thereby express the attitude he so ascribed, nor would he speak with first-person authority about it. ("I unconsciously want to gain weight" is an expression of *opinion about* a desire; it's not an expression of desire.)

I have argued that by giving the right sort of attention to the expressive dimension of psychological self-ascriptions we can make sense of, among other things, first-person authority. Max is able to express his desire for, say, a bite of ravioli *either* by reaching across the table for a bite or by saying, "I want a bite of ravioli." Once we get this (mundane) fact into proper focus, we are in a position to understand (1) why Max needn't consult evidence about himself when he speaks about his own desires (he needn't consult evidence before he reaches across the table either) and (2) why, if I wish to learn what Max wants, *he* is probably the best person for me to ask (*his* expressive nonverbal behavior is also the best expressive nonverbal behavior for me to watch). Earlier, I noted that according to Moran, "A proper philosophical account of self-knowledge should tell us how it is that a person can speak about his own mind, without appealing to evidence about himself," where his not appealing to evidence "contributes rather than detracts from the authority of what he says" (2001, 135). One of my aims in this book has been to offer such an account.

ABBREVIATIONS USED IN THIS BOOK

REFERENCES

INDEX

Abbreviations Used in This Book

B&B   Wittgenstein, L. *The Blue and the Brown Books.* New York: Harper and Row, 1958.

LWPP1   Wittgenstein, L. *Last Writings on the Philosophy of Psychology,* vol. 1. Tr. C. G. Luckhardt and M. A. E. Aue. Ed. G. H. von Wright and H. Nyman. Chicago: University of Chicago Press, 1982.

LWPP2   Wittgenstein, L. *Last Writings on the Philosophy of Psychology,* vol. 2. Tr. C. G. Luckhardt and M. A. E. Aue. Ed. G. H. von Wright and H. Nyman. Oxford: Blackwell, 1992.

OC   Wittgenstein, L. *On Certainty.* Tr. D. Paul and G. E. M. Anscombe. Ed. G. E. M. Anscombe and G. H. von Wright. New York: Harper and Row, 1969.

PI   Wittgenstein, L. *Philosophical Investigations.* Tr. G. E. M. Anscombe. New York: Macmillan Publishing Co., Inc., 1958.

PR   Wittgenstein, L. *Philosophical Remarks.* Tr. R. Hargreaves and R. White. Ed. R. Rhees. Chicago: University of Chicago Press, 1975.

RPP2   Wittgenstein, L. *Remarks on the Philosophy of Psychology,* vol. 2. Tr. C. G. Luckhardt and M. A. E. Aue. Ed. G. H. von Wright and H. Nyman. Chicago: University of Chicago Press, 1980.

Z   Wittgenstein, L. *Zettel.* Tr. G. E. M. Anscombe. Ed. G. E. M. Anscombe and G. H. von Wright. Berkeley: University of California Press, 1981.

References

Alston, W. P. 1967. "Expressing." In *Philosophy in America*. Ed. M. Black. Ithaca, NY: Cornell University Press.

Armstrong, D. M. 1968. *A Materialist Theory of Mind*. London: Routledge and Kegan Paul.

Armstrong, D. M., and Malcolm, N. 1984. *Consciousness and Causality*. Oxford: Blackwell.

Ayer, A. J. 1946. *Language, Truth, and Logic*. London: Victor Gollancz.

Baker, G., and Hacker, P. 1984. *Scepticism, Rules and Language*. Oxford: Basil Blackwell.

Bloor, D. 1983. *Wittgenstein: A Social Theory of Knowledge*. New York: Columbia University Press.

Boghossian, P. A. 1989. "The Rule-Following Considerations," *Mind*, 98: 508–549.

Brentano, F. 1973. *Psychology from an Empirical Standpoint*. Tr. Antos C. Rancurello, D. B. Terrell, and Linda L. McAlister. Ed. O. Kraus. London: Routledge and Kegan Paul.

Breuer, J., and Freud, S. 2000. *Studies on Hysteria*. Tr. and ed. J. Strachey and A. Freud. New York: Basic Books.

Byrne, A. 1996. "On Misinterpreting Kripke's Wittgenstein," *Philosophy and Phenomenological Research*, 56 (June): 339–343.

Churchland, P. 1984. *Matter and Consciousness*. Cambridge, MA: MIT Press.

Collins, A. 1969. "Unconscious Belief," *Journal of Philosophy*, 66 (October 16): 667–680.

Comte, A. 1974. *The Essential Comte*. Tr. Margaret Clarke. New York: Barnes and Noble Books.

Davidson, D. 1980. "Mental Events." In *Essays on Actions and Events*. Oxford: Oxford University Press.

—— 1986. "A Coherence Theory of Truth and Knowledge." In *Truth and Interpretation: Perspectives on the Philosophy of Donald Davidson.* Ed. E. LePore. Basil Blackwell: Oxford.

Diamond, C. 1991. *The Realistic Spirit.* Cambridge, MA: MIT Press.

Evans, G. 1982. *The Varieties of Reference.* Ed. John McDowell. Oxford: Oxford University Press.

Finkelstein, D. H. 1994. "Speaking My Mind: First-Person Authority and Conscious Mentality." Ph.D. diss., University of Pittsburgh.

——. 1999a. "On the Distinction between Conscious and Unconscious States of Mind," *American Philosophical Quarterly* 36 (April): 79–100.

——. 1999b. "On Self-Blindness and Inner Sense," *Philosophical Topics* 26 (Spring & Fall): 105–119.

Fogelin, R. J. 1987. *Wittgenstein.* London: Routledge.

Frege, G. 1952. *Translations from the Philosophical Writings of Gottlob Frege.* Totowa, NJ: Rowman and Littlefield.

——. 1953. *The Foundations of Arithmetic.* Evanston, IL: Northwestern University Press.

Freud, S. 1966. *Introductory Lectures on Psychoanalysis.* Tr. and ed. James Strachey. New York: W. W. Norton.

Goldfarb, W. 1985. "Kripke on Wittgenstein and Rules," *Journal of Philosophy,* 82: 471–488.

Humphrey, N. 1986. *The Inner Eye.* London: Faber and Faber, Ltd.

Hylton, P. 1990. *Russell, Idealism and the Emergence of Analytic Philosophy.* Oxford: Oxford University Press.

James, W. 1890. *The Principles of Psychology.* New York: Henry Holt and Company.

Kripke, S. A. 1982. *Wittgenstein on Rules and Private Language.* Cambridge, MA: Harvard University Press.

Leibniz, G. W. 1981. *New Essays on Human Understanding.* Tr. and ed. P. Remnant and J. Bennett. Cambridge: Cambridge University Press.

Lycan, W. 1996. *Consciousness and Experience.* Cambridge, MA: MIT Press.

McDowell, J. 1996. *Mind and World.* Cambridge, MA: Harvard University Press.

——. 1998a. "Having the World in View: Sellars, Kant, and Intentionality," *Journal of Philosophy,* 95: 431–491.

——. 1998b. "Intentionality and Interiority in Wittgenstein." In *Mind, Value, and Reality.* Cambridge, MA: Harvard University Press.

——. 1998c. "Meaning and Intentionality in Wittgenstein's Later Philosophy." In *Mind, Value, and Reality.* Cambridge: Harvard University Press.

——. 1998d. "One Strand in the Private Language Argument." In *Mind, Value, and Reality.* Cambridge, MA: Harvard University Press.

———. 1998e. "Response to Crispin Wright." In *Knowing Our Own Minds.* Ed. C. Wright, B. C. Smith, and C. Macdonald. Oxford: Oxford University Press.

———. 1998f. "Wittgenstein on Following a Rule." In *Mind, Value, and Reality.* Cambridge, MA: Harvard University Press.

McGinn, C. 1979. "Action and Its Explanation." In *Philosophical Problems in Psychology.* Ed. N. Bolton. New York: Methuen and Co.

———. 1984. *Wittgenstein on Meaning.* Oxford: Basil Blackwell.

Mellor, D. H. 1977–78. "Conscious Belief," *Proceedings of the Aristotelian Society,* 78: 87–101.

Mill, J. S. 1961. *Auguste Comte and Positivism.* Ann Arbor: University of Michigan Press.

Moran, R. 1997. "Self-Knowledge: Discovery, Resolution, and Undoing," *European Journal of Philosophy,* 5 (August): 141–161.

———. 2001. *Authority and Estrangement: An Essay on Self-Knowledge.* Princeton, NJ: Princeton University Press.

Price, H. H. 1932. *Perception.* London: Methuen and Co. Ltd.

Rey, G. 1988. "Toward a Computational Account of *Akrasia* and Self-Deception." In *Perspectives on Self-Deception.* Ed. B. P. McLaughlin and A. O. Rorty. Berkeley: University of California Press.

Rorty, R. 1979. *Philosophy and the Mirror of Nature.* Princeton: Princeton University Press.

———. 1991. "Freud and Moral Reflection." In *Essays on Heidegger and Others: Philosophical Papers,* vol. 2. Cambridge: Cambridge University Press.

Rosenthal, D. 1993. "Thinking That One Thinks." In *Consciousness.* Ed. M. Davies and G. W. Humphreys. Oxford: Basil Blackwell.

Russell, B. 1912. *The Problems of Philosophy.* Oxford: Oxford University Press.

———. 1917. "The Relation of Sense-Data to Physics." In *Mysticism and Logic.* Totowa, NJ: Barnes and Noble Books.

———. 1921. *The Analysis of Mind.* New York: Humanities Press.

———. 1992. *Theory of Knowledge: The 1913 Manuscript.* Ed. E. R. Eames. London: Routledge.

Searle, J. 1992. *The Rediscovery of the Mind.* Cambridge, MA: MIT Press.

Sellars, W. 1997. *Empiricism and the Philosophy of Mind.* Cambridge, MA: Harvard University Press.

Shoemaker, S. 1988. "On Knowing One's Own Mind." In *Philosophical Perspectives,* vol. 2, *Epistemology:* 183–209.

———. 1994. "Self-Knowledge and 'Inner Sense', Lecture II: The Broad Perceptual Model." *Philosophy and Phenomenological Research,* 54 (2): 271–290.

Strawson, P. 1966. *The Bounds of Sense.* London: Methuen and Co.

Tait, W. W. 1986. "Truth and Proof: The Platonism of Mathematics," *Synthese,* 69: 341–370.

Thompson, M. n.d. "Naive Action Theory." Unpublished manuscript.

Wilson, G. M. 1998. "Semantic Realism and Kripke's Wittgenstein," *Philosophy and Phenomenological Research,* 58 (March): 99–122.

Wittgenstein, L. 1922. *Tractatus Logico-Philosophicus.* Tr. C. K. Ogden. London: Routledge and Kegan Paul.

———. 1958a. *The Blue and Brown Books.* New York: Harper and Row, 1958.

———. 1958b. *Philosophical Investigations.* Tr. G. E. M. Anscombe. New York: Macmillan Publishing Co.

———. 1969. *On Certainty.* Tr. D. Paul and G. E. M. Anscombe. Ed. G. E. M. Anscombe and G. H. von Wright. New York: Harper and Row.

———. 1975. *Philosophical Remarks.* Tr. R. Hargreaves and R. White. Ed. R. Rhees. Chicago: University of Chicago Press.

———. 1980. *Remarks on the Philosophy of Psychology,* vol. 2. Tr. C. G. Luckhardt and M. A. E. Aue. Ed. G. H. von Wright and H. Nyman. Chicago: University of Chicago Press.

———. 1981. *Zettel.* Tr. G. E. M. Anscombe. Ed. G. E. M. Anscombe and G. H. von Wright. Berkeley: University of California Press.

———. 1982. *Last Writings on the Philosophy of Psychology,* vol. 1. Tr. C. G. Luckhardt and M. A. E. Aue. Ed. G. H. von Wright and H. Nyman. Chicago: University of Chicago Press.

———. 1992. *Last Writings on the Philosophy of Psychology,* vol. 2. Tr. C. G. Luckhardt and M. A. E. Aue. Ed. G. H. von Wright and H. Nyman. Oxford: Blackwell.

Wright, C. 1998. "Self-Knowledge: The Wittgensteinian Legacy." In *Knowing Our Own Minds.* Ed. C. Wright, B. C. Smith, and C. Macdonald. Oxford: Oxford University Press.

———. 2001a. "Excerpts from a Critical Study of Colin McGinn's *Wittgenstein on Meaning.*" In *Rails to Infinity: Essays on Themes from Wittgenstein's* Philosophical Investigations. Cambridge, MA: Harvard University Press.

———. 2001b. "On Making Up One's Mind: Wittgenstein on Intention." In *Rails to Infinity: Essays on Themes from Wittgenstein's* Philosophical Investigations. Cambridge, MA: Harvard University Press.

———. 2001c. "The Problem of Self-Knowledge (II)." In *Rails to Infinity: Essays on Themes from Wittgenstein's* Philosophical Investigations. Cambridge, MA: Harvard University Press.

———. 2001d. "Study Note on Wittgenstein on the Nature of Philosophy and Its Proper Method." In *Rails to Infinity: Essays on Themes from Witt-*

genstein's Philosophical Investigations. Cambridge, MA: Harvard University Press.

———. 2001e. "Wittgenstein's Rule-Following Considerations and the Central Project of Theoretical Linguistics." In *Rails to Infinity: Essays on Themes from Wittgenstein's* Philosophical Investigations. Cambridge, MA: Harvard University Press.

Index

Alston, W. P., 95–96
Anger, 20–23, 25–26, 116–117, 119, 120n, 122, 125
Animals, 6, 26n, 64–66, 128–129, 143–148. *See also* Dogs
Armstrong, D. M., 17, 18n, 19n, 20n, 65–66
Army colonel, 28, 38n, 102
Assertion. *See* Expression
Avowal, 5, 25–26, 29n, 37, 39, 44, 46–49, 52, 61–62, 75, 92–99, 100–101, 103, 104n, 111, 113, 123–125, 132–134, 137, 141, 144n, 145–146, 153; Moran on, 158, 160–165, 167. *See also* Constitutivism
Ayer, A. J., 95n

Baker, G., 34n
Behavior: as evidence for psychological ascriptions, 16, 23, 26, 100–103, 120, 123–124, 126, 133, 155; understood as divested of psychological significance, 44, 90–93. *See also* Expression; First-person authority
Belief, 1, 2, 17, 26, 45, 47–50, 64, 100, 110, 115–121, 153–159, 166; perceptual, 55–59; compared with sensation, 64, 127, 147–148. *See also* Constitutivism; Judgment
Blindsight, 24
Bloor, D., 87n
Boghossian, P., 34n

Brain, 18, 19n, 24n, 26
Brentano, F., 11
Byrne, A., 34n

"Can't help but," 48
CEO, 104–110, 126
Churchland, P., 17–18
Coherentism, 54, 56–57
Collins, A., 121n
Comte, A., 10
Concepts/conceptual capacities, 26n, 53–61, 63–72, 106, 129, 131–133, 136–137, 141–144, 146–148, 150, 156–158
Consciousness/conscious vs. unconscious, 2, 4, 6, 9, 11–12, 16–24, 26–27, 66, 100, 114–127, 129, 143–145, 148, 154, 164–165, 166n, 167n, 168; occurrent item in, 64, 66, 68, 71, 75, 127, 129, 131, 158, 162
Constitutivism, 2–4, 28–50, 51–53, 61–62, 75, 90–93, 153–154; belief-, 38n, 45, 47–48, 50, 61; avowal-, 38n, 45–49, 52, 61
Context/context principle, 92, 106–108, 110, 141
Customs and institutions, 87

Davidson, D., 56–57, 150n
Deliberation, 153, 159–167
Descartes, R., 17, 18, 64
Desire, 1, 12, 15–16, 33, 37–38, 43–45,

179

Desire *(continued)*
51, 89–90, 110, 115n, 123, 125–126,
143–144, 153, 155–158, 160–161, 163–
164, 166, 168; contrast with belief,
157–158, 166
Detectivism, 2–3, 9–27, 28–29, 50, 51–
52, 62, 75, 139n, 153–155, 158, 165;
new detectivism, 10, 13, 15–19, 22–23,
27, 60–62, 71–72, 125, 139n; old
detectivism, 10, 13–15, 22–23, 27, 51–
52, 62–75, 139n
Diamond, C., 140, 146
Dogs, 64–65, 129, 143, 146–147, 163,
165; wet "doggy," 67–71. *See also* Phantom smell
Dreams, 112
Dualism, 13–14, 27
Dylan, B., 1–2, 5

Emotivism, 95
Eroom's paradox, 118–119, 121
Evans, G., 69–70, 154–156, 159
Expectation, 4–5, 82, 91–93, 99, 111,
113, 126, 128
Expression, 5, 65, 75, 84, 88–99, 100–
101, 103–105, 109–113, 142, 144–148,
168; and assertion, 5, 93, 95–99; facial,
90–91, 97, 101; and consciousness,
119–124; of sensation, 130, 134–135,
137–138, 139n, 141. *See also*
Wittgenstein, L.
Expressivism, 5, 93–99

Fear, 1, 2, 49, 65, 66, 68, 75, 159–160, 166
Fiddler on the Roof, 122–123, 125
Finkelstein, D. H., 19n, 120n, 122n,
144n, 158n
First-person authority, 1–2, 6, 75, 98–99,
148; and consciousness, 4, 20–23, 26–
27, 119, 167–168; three-paragraph account of, 100–106, 113–114; about behavior, 102–104, 109–114, 126; about
thought, 103–104, 112–114; about
meaning, 104–110; degrees of, 108,
124–125; detectivist approach to (*see*
Detectivism); constitutivist approach
to (*see* Constitutivism); middle path
account of (*see* Middle path account);
transparency approach to (*see* Transparency)

Fogelin, R. J., 98–99
Franny and Zooey, 102–103, 109–113,
126–127
Frege, G., 106–110
Freud, S., 114n, 121–122

Given. *See* Myth of the Given
Goldfarb, W., 35n
Grammar, 69, 85, 130, 137–141, 145
Grief, 84n, 91, 111

Hacker, P., 34n
Harry, 115–121, 123–125
Helen, 123–125
Humphrey, N., 18
Hunger, 15, 163
Hylton, P., 14

Inner sense, 2, 3, 10–14, 16–19, 23–27,
72, 116, 133, 155–158, 160, 166;
McDowell on, 58–61, 63, 135, 141. *See
also* Detectivism
Intention, 1–2, 5, 9, 18, 25, 28, 37n, 38n,
75, 85n, 100, 142, 145–146, 153–154;
unconscious vs. conscious, 22–23, 114,
119, 121, 122n; and rule-following,
33–38, 41, 43, 44; responsibility and
avowal of, 45–46, 49–50, 52; compared with sensation, 62–63, 64, 69,
142n; and deliberation, 158, 159n,
160–161, 163n, 165–168
Interpretation, 30–33, 36, 37n, 40–44,
45, 76–77, 79–83, 87, 89, 91, 105–111,
113, 139n
Intimacy, 51–53, 62–63, 72, 154
Introspection. *See* Inner sense

James, W., 11
Jealousy, 20–21, 23–25, 116, 123,
163
Jekyll, Dr., 114
Joke, 1, 102–103, 151
Judgment, 2, 36–37, 38n, 39, 44, 45, 69,
77–78, 83, 85n, 88, 98, 120n, 129, 149,
159n; and perceptual experience, 53–
62, 132–135
Justification, 34–35, 54–56, 58–62,
66–68, 70–72, 87, 115, 124n, 125n,
127, 128, 133–136, 145, 148–152,
161